Praise for Kerry Dunnington's *Tasting the Seasons*

"Kerry has a heartfelt commitment to eating local and in season, and helping us all to develop a real sense of ethics toward our home here on this planet—the only home we have!"

—John Shields, Chef, National PBS-TV Host, Author

"Dunnington has a unique way of profiling and combining unlikely ingredients that make her recipes appealing. With the greatest of ease, she folds in helpful tips, techniques and passion for what she is preparing."

—Molly Kushner, Whole Foods Market

"...a wondrous cookbook for those who are interested in seasonal eating, locally sourced food, and ways to affect the way you shop and select ingredients. Whether or not you enjoy cooking, this book is not only a good read but designed in a clear and easy-to-follow format....a reliable resource for everyday use, but also a great gift for any cook who appreciates an inspired as well as informational approach to preparing, serving and enjoying wonderful and healthy food creations."

—Kater Leatherman, *OutLook by the Bay* magazine

"Kerry has a nose for what's new in the food world, and she always incorporates the new with the tried and true to create truly fabulous recipes that are clear and easy to follow."

—Hope Keller, former editor, *Smart Woman* magazine

"...sure to become your eco-classic resource to get you back cooking in the kitchen and supporting local agriculture."

—Joan Norman, One Straw Farm

"I offer my most enthusiastic recommendation for *baltimore eats* longtime columnist, Kerry Dunnington. The feedback from her popular column, 'A Reason for the Season' is a testament to her engaging stories and mouth-watering recipes."

—Bonnie North, former chapter leader, Slow Food Baltimore

"I love this cookbook because there are great everyday recipes using ingredients that are readily available. The fact that Kerry has focused on using local ingredients as well as more fish than meat is also great for a modern lifestyle. I loved the first book, *This Book Cooks,* which has become my go-to book for inspiration, but I can see this book being an additional great resource!"

—Izzy Zarrillo

"The recipes I've prepared are absolutely delicious. They are easy to prepare, yet sophisticated enough for a discerning palate. Containing just the right novel yet simple ingredients to impress your guests! The recipes I've tried so far prove that good, healthy food doesn't require an exhaustive list of expensive ingredients, break the budget or take hours to prepare. The brief, user friendly and easy to read chapters listing eco-terms and tips, carefully and intelligently vetted product and ingredient information, and her entertaining advice displays the author's wisdom, humor and common sense when it comes to food and life! If you're looking to improve the health of yourself and those you love as well as the health of the planet, Kerry Dunnington, sets out to make it tasty, surprisingly easy and yes, enjoyable. Even for a time-challenged mother like myself!"

—Karen Goco, Mom

"My friend introduced me to this wonderful book because she knows that I love healthy foods and believe in simple cooking. Yes, yummy food and easy cooking are not contradictory, which this book shows. I have also watched Kerry's YouTube, visited her blog and will encourage others to do the same while enjoying her book. Nowadays there are too many choices we have to indulge ourselves in unhealthy eating habits, we really need more of such books to teach ourselves and help our kids to develop a healthy eating style which they can benefit for a lifetime."

—**Sparkly, Fairfax, VA**

"Cooking has never been something I do for pleasure but out of necessity. With this book (it's much more than just a cookbook), I really enjoy the process of preparing food for the first time in my life. This book is as much a philosophy as it is a collection of recipes. With its environmentally friendly focus and straightforward presentation, it's not only easy to follow but a pleasure to read. Dunnington not only provides definitions and pronunciations but shares links on where to purchase suggested items (everything from produce to cast-iron cookware) and truly helpful tips on what to look for when buying produce and suggestions on how to use specific ingredients. There's also a really helpful Product Resource List in the back which makes it all seem easy, which with this book it really is."

—**J. Miller, Morrisville, PA**

"I bought this cookbook for my wife. Food is great! Highly recommend the French onion soup and who knew there were so many ways to make a meatloaf, much less with meatless ingredients as an option. Healthy, comfort food."

—**Bogey Boggs**

"...many wonderful easy recipes for someone like me who is not a cook. The classic meatloaf was outstanding along with the roasted Romano red potatoes. Also tried the crab cakes and loved them."

—**Gail Koch**

"...this one's a keeper...clearly, the author is a well-informed, experienced kitchenmeister and hostess, also passionate about what's good for our health and our planet. Contents are interesting, easy to read, easy to use, and scrumptious."

—**Elizabeth Somerville**

TASTING THE SEASONS

ALSO BY KERRY DUNNINGTON

This Book Cooks

TASTING THE SEASONS

Inspired, In-Season Cuisine That's Easy,
Healthy, Fresh and Fun

KERRY DUNNINGTON

Artichoke Publishers
Baltimore, Maryland

Artichoke Publishers
220 Stoneyford Road
Baltimore, Maryland 21210
www.kerrydunnington.com

Cover art by Elizabeth Cockey. Cover and interior design by Anita Jones, Another Jones Graphics. Interior illustrations by Sheryl Southwick.

Publisher's Cataloging-In-Publication Data
(Prepared by The Donohue Group, Inc.)

Dunnington, Kerry.
    Tasting the seasons : inspired, in-season cuisine that's easy, healthy, fresh and fun / Kerry Dunnington.

    pages ; cm

    Includes bibliographical references and index.
    ISBN: 978-0-9904185-0-4

    1. Seasonal cooking. 2. Cookery (Natural foods) 3. One-dish meals. 4. Nutrition. 5. Cookbooks. I. Title.

TX840.S43 D86 2014
641.5/64

Manufactured and printed in the United States of America

DEDICATION

To Nick and Caramel, my two greatest loves.

To Joan Leatherman D'Angelo.
Her love of cooking was rivaled only by her love of sharing.
My mother. My culinary mentor.

In memory of Lorrayne Paulette Shumaker and my father,
Edward Gordon Leatherman.

ACKNOWLEDGEMENTS

I am grateful to all the people who helped to test and retest the recipes that appear in this cookbook, especially Nick, my official taste-tester and husband extraordinaire. My gratitude also extends to many family, friends, readers and supporters—everyone who has helped make my career in "all things food" be all things wonderful!

I also want to share my thanks to my serendipitous friend, Jennifer Alterwitz, to Kate Gallagher (a lifelong friend whom it took years to meet), and yet another, Martha Lucius, for her expertise and time. And enormous thanks to Alix Cochrane Rodman— I can't look at this cookbook and not think about her generosity and patience, and the time she devoted to this project.

To my nephews and nieces—Izzy, Ian, Sean, Travis, Connor, Garrett and Keelinn—I hope that in some way I've helped to instill good, healthy eating habits in each of you and that you'll pass on the eco-torch to future generations for the betterment of our planet.

About the illustrator: Sheryl Southwick is an accomplished artist who loves drawing and all endeavors it can lead to, including painting, mosaic making, printmaking, and the creation of multi-media interactive pieces. Cooking is her favorite thing to do on Sundays. Her website is www.sherylsouthwick.com.

CONTENTS

Introducing

TASTING THE SEASONS

Tasting the Seasons rests on my belief that the most delicious, healthy meals are made from fresh, seasonal, pesticide-free food supplied by local farmers who are committed to sustainable practices. My goal in creating this book was to provide a readable and entertaining blueprint to help you prepare flavorful dishes "from scratch"—following food seasons, appreciating nature's bounty and sharing with family and friends.

What sets *Tasting the Seasons* apart from many volumes in this genre are my personal insights and anecdotes drawn from my life-long culinary journey. These stories reflect my dedication to my readers' health and to the well-being of Planet Earth, and I hope they enhance the credibility of my varied and user-friendly recipes, which include family-oriented one-dish wonders, updated classics, creative gourmet entrees, and fast, fresh, easy meals.

During my three decades of cooking, catering, research and writing, I have developed two key values in preparing fresh food—it must be seasonal and it must be innovative. These are the values that prevail in *Tasting the Seasons.*

The book is designed to help you understand the importance of knowing where food comes from and how you can make healthy and sustainable food choices. It also conveys the powerful benefits of serving food that is whole, real, seasonal, local and well-prepared. My purpose is not only to provide excellent recipes, but to transform the way you—and your family and friends— feel about preparing and eating great-tasting food.

Today's tremendous renewed interest in traditional cooking with locally-produced ingredients makes now the perfect time for *Tasting the Seasons.* Thanks to the exploding knowledge and awareness of how diet affects health, millions of Americans are turning away from fast, inexpensive and unhealthy food choices, looking instead for farm-fresh and home-prepared. At the same time, thanks to greater concern for the environment, we are reducing our fast-food indulgences (and their wasteful packaging) in favor of home-cooked meals, served with eco-friendly, china, glass and flatware. Whether shared around your formal dining room table or at your kitchen counter, the meals you cook at home are much more likely to be nutritious and satisfying—as well as far less taxing on your budget and the environment—than store-bought, carry-out, drive-thru or prepared food.

I do hope that *Tasting the Seasons* makes cooking and entertaining in your home easy, healthy, interesting and fun—for you and for your family and friends.

Kerry

ENTERTAINING

Nick and I love to entertain, although I must admit that some of our earlier attempts were not what you'd call smooth sailing. Suffice it to say, with a couple of decades of entertaining under our belts along with the invaluable experiences I've had as a caterer, we can host a party for eight or seventy-eight … relatively glitch-free. You, too, can throw a successful party, but before I give you the how-tos, there are three key to-dos that only you can implement:

- Plan ahead.
- Keep an ongoing to-do list.
- Do everything that needs doing.

Begin your party planning by setting a date, creating your guest list, and sending invitations.

Menu

Begin by planning a menu, (or hire a caterer who will do it all, see below) making sure thought is given to the number of dishes you can prepare in advance and how many dishes require cooking time and/or your time spent in the kitchen during the life of the party. Make the menu festive, seasonal, well-rounded, and colorful. I recommend hiring party staff. This frees you up to spend time with your guests, and party helpers do all the serving, clearing and general party clean up.

If you decide to hire a caterer, make sure it's one whose profile matches the type of party you're hosting. Some caterers are better suited for weddings; some are better suited for intimate private-home parties. Also, know that there are many levels of service that a good caterer can offer you. As a rule, the best way to find a caterer is by word of mouth. Choose the catering company that catered the party you most enjoyed as a guest.

The Bar

Providing a full bar entails having scotch, vodka, gin, bourbon, rum, assorted wines, and beers plus mixers and cocktail fruit. If you're hosting a large party, a full bar should also entail the hiring of a bartender. Keep the bar area clean, replenishing ice, cocktail fruit, napkins and glasses. If you want to enjoy your party, I recommend hiring staff.

If bringing in a bartender doesn't fit within your budget, you don't have to be wedded to serving the complexities of a full bar. Limit the offerings to assorted wines, beers and non-alcoholic beverages, and arrange the bar area to be self-serve. Or take it a step further and keep the liquid refreshment options simple; serve Seasonal Sangria (see page 44) and one or two additional beverages. The other option is to design a bar menu to go with the type of party you're hosting. For brunch, a mimosa, Bloody Mary and coffee bar is perfect. For a luncheon, you can serve Hibiscus Tea over Candied Ginger Ice (see page 43) along with complementary wine and sparkling water.

If you choose any of these streamlined bar options, display a bar menu on the serving table. It's simple to create and print yourself; or you may opt for a more personal and distinct look and simply write it by hand. A bar menu is a very nice, detailed touch that announces the drinks you're serving and helps to cut down on guests asking if there's a full bar elsewhere.

Party Staff
The first time Nick and I hosted a large cocktail party (about seventy-five people) was after we moved into our current home. We planned and executed a fabulous menu and provided guests with a full bar. What we didn't think to provide was a bartender or party helpers, and oh, were we sorry. The two of us were running around like jackrabbits, trying to be the perfect hosts: receiving coats and hostess gifts, mixing drinks, replenishing ice and glasses, pulling this and that from the oven, refreshing food items, all the while trying to be calm and conversational. It's no wonder we've never hosted another party where we haven't secured staff. Party helpers come with varying degrees of experience, from chef to kitchen help to bartender to servers. They're an invaluable asset as they enhance your presence as a host or hostess, allowing you the ability to relax and enjoy the company of your guests.

Party Planning Pointers
Beverages, quick-chilling – If you've forgotten to chill the beer and wine, nearly fill the bucket/container you will be serving the bottles from with ice and salted cold water: one tablespoon of salt for each quart of cold water. Set the beer and/or wine in the ice mixture.

Candles – I love candlelight; it illuminates a room in such a beautiful way and makes the atmosphere in your home warm and inviting. But for your health and the health of the environment, take caution when buying traditional wax candles which are made of toxic petroleum-based paraffin. Paraffin, when burned, produces carcinogens and soot, and soot contains many of the same toxins produced by burning diesel fuel. The healthy alternative is to buy candles made from beeswax and/or soy. These candles contain only plant-based agents, they're free of synthetic fragrances, paraffin and petroleum bi-products and they burn free of toxic soot. When buying beeswax or soy candles, make certain the label clearly states they are made from 100% beeswax and/or soy; I've discovered that some contain small amounts of paraffin. Soy ranks higher on the environmentally friendly scale than beeswax; soy is the cleanest burning wax. If you have any trouble finding these candles locally, check the internet for a variety of options.

Centerpieces – When planning and setting the table for a sit-down dinner party, consideration should be given to the height of the centerpiece. Whether it's a piece of art or a flower arrangement, it is best if the centerpiece doesn't prohibit guests from seeing one another. If fresh flowers are not within your budget, decorate with seasonal fruits and vegetables, fresh herbs and nuts. This is a great way to further utilize the season's bounty, and it allows your décor to do double duty. After your party is over, you can use your centerpieces in recipes. Below are some natural centerpiece suggestions, one for each season.

SUMMER

Arrange fresh summer herbs in a short, wide-mouth mason jar and wrap ribbon (whatever festive ribbon matches your theme and/or décor) around the mouth of the jar. This is not only beautiful, the aroma is divine. Post-party, dry the herbs for use in your favorite recipes.

FALL

For a festive centerpiece, arrange an assortment of pumpkins, pomegranates, winter squash, apples, pears, and nuts. Turn your centerpiece into many of the recipes in *Tasting the Seasons* that make use of the fall harvest.

WINTER

Place fresh, whole cranberries in the bottom of a clear glass vessel, and instead of flowers, arrange small red or white Swiss chard leaves along with any other hardy greens. Assemble just prior to the arrival of your guests. Turn the cranberries into Raspberry Orange Cranberry Sauce (see page 38), then sauté the greens and serve as a side dish.

SPRING

Blanch fresh asparagus spears for a few minutes or until they turn a brightly-colored grass green. Arrange them in a lattice pattern atop a white platter and creatively dot the surface of the platter with Easter egg radishes, keeping their tops intact. Your asparagus can then be used in Asparagus Soup and the radishes can be used for either Leafy Greens with Radish and Eggs or Rainbow Radish Rice (see Index for recipes).

Menu cards

Menu cards generally adorn all my tables, whether it's a party I'm catering or one I'm hosting. People love to know what's on the menu, and they really appreciate this intimate, personalized detail. You can print menu cards using a computer and printer or you can write them by hand. I prefer to use the same paper stock for my menu cards as I used for my invitations (www. thepapermillstore.com).

Place cards

Place cards at seated parties add a lovely touch to the table, especially if the cards you've selected (handmade or store-bought) are in keeping with the theme, season, and/or décor. Place cards also allow guests to locate their seat while the host is finalizing the meal, rather than having everyone wondering and, worse, asking where they should sit.

There are some positive and negative factors to place cards. It's important to know whom you're placing with whom; it can make all the difference in the outcome of this intimate-style party. Boy-girl-boy-girl doesn't always work, and some couples prefer to sit together, while others do not. It's always best to seat compatible people across from each other rather than next to each other; it makes for a better flow of conversation.

While there are a multitude of places to buy place cards, my favorite online store is Beau-coup Favors. I like their eco-friendly plantable seed place cards and the conversational party topics place cards.

RSVP – From the French: Répondez S'il Vous Plaît.
The English translation: Reply if you please or simply … Please reply.

As a frequent party giver, I can't stress enough the importance of knowing how many of your invited guests will be attending. Social graces seem to have gone by the wayside. Etiquette is for another book; let's focus on how you can try to get your guests to respond to an RSVP.

- Always provide a deadline for their reply. A respond-by date implies that this is an organized, detailed party. Be specific as to the person they are responding to; give them a name, phone number and email address.
- If you haven't heard back from a guest and an accurate head-count is important, go ahead and call them. Don't make them feel guilty; an I-hope-you'll-be-here should work.

Serving pieces, utensils and skewers
The utensils you choose for serving are important, especially for a buffet dinner party. I've stood in buffet lines that were held up by people having trouble navigating food to their plates. The proper serving pieces will make a difference in the flow of your buffet line.

Pick On Us sells my favorite knotted bamboo skewer (www.pickonus.com). Made from all natural bamboo, they're not only eco-friendly, they're also elegant. Pick On Us currently offers a variety of all-natural bamboo picks, stirrers and skewers. They also have reusable serving spoons and forks as well as disposable plates and flatware.

Serving sizes
It's hard to gauge appetites (especially when entertaining); therefore, serving sizes can be tricky. When you're planning a party menu, a general rule that works for me is about one generous handful of fruits and vegetables per person and at least four to six ounces of protein. Allow more for teenage boys; their appetites are voracious. For second helpings, prepare about half the total amount. So, if you're serving green beans to ten people, you will need ten generous handfuls plus an additional five generous handfuls for second helpings: a total of fifteen generous handfuls. As with most elements of entertaining, it's important to know your guests: the ones with hearty appetites as well as the ones who will be full after eating a handful of peanuts.

THE 365 CHALLENGE

The idea of The 365 Challenge is that you and your family, your friends and your neighbors, your classmates, book club, garden club and yoga class, come up with ways to challenge each other in order to help save our planet. Whether it's for one day, one week, one month or one year, every conscious change helps when you're cutting back on non-recyclable, eco-unfriendly, man-made materials. Be aware of what you're buying and using.

Down with Plastic Challenge:

Try to resist putting anything plastic into your grocery cart, and before checking out ... remove any plastic that might have snuck in there.

In-Out Challenge:

Only bring in something new to replace the broken or worn out. Buy only what you need.

No Boxes, No Cans Challenge:

Buy only fresh foods, nothing in a box or can. Try to grocery shop without going down an aisle.

Eat-In Challenge:

If fast food, eat-out, drive-thru is your lifestyle, make a change and eat in. But instead of eating store-bought or getting home delivery, use only fresh ingredients and make at least one dish from scratch.

Home State Challenge:

Try not to buy anything that comes from out of state or from another country. Be aware of where your food is coming from. Read labels and stickers. Buy locally.

New Food of the Week Challenge:

Introduce a new fruit, vegetable, grain, bean, even a new herb or spice to your family or yourself. Buy something you don't know how to pronounce or that you've never eaten before.

Introducing

APPETIZERS

Based on the style of party you're hosting, there are two types of appetizers to choose from: stationary and what I like to call one-bite-no-drip walkabouts. Stationary appetizers are best to serve when hosting small, intimate parties where guests are seated together in one room. These are typically elaborate (sometimes drippy) appetizers that can be more challenging to eat and may require a small plate and fork. The one-bite-no-drip walkabout appetizer is best served when hosting larger parties (i.e. cocktail parties and buffet dinner parties) where the appetizers will likely be butlered and where guests will likely be mingling. Often, guests at these parties are negotiating a crowd with a glass in hand. Awkward-size food or drippy bites are not recommended for a large party.

You'll find plenty of both types of appetizers within this section. Many of them can be prepared in advance, some with just a little last-minute heating required. When designing your appetizer menu, consideration should be given to the entire menu; appetizers should complement your main meal. For example, if a significant amount of cheese is in the main entrée, don't overload and serve cheese as an appetizer.

As much as I encourage eating fresh vegetables, seldom will I prepare the omnipresent raw vegetable platter as an appetizer. At the risk of sounding immodest, I compare the pre-packaged cut-up veggies under plastic (found everywhere) to store-bought dressing; we can do so much better for ourselves, our families, and our guests. On the other hand, if you feel like your party isn't complete without crudités, here are a few unique ways to serve raw vegetables.

Creative Crudités

- Remove tops from red, yellow and/or orange peppers; stand cooked (until just fork tender), cold asparagus spears inside the peppers, tip side up.

- For a stunning presentation, serve steamed (until slightly crisp) snow peas on a bed of ice cubes. (The smaller the cubes, the more dramatic the presentation.)

- Alternately skewer pitted black olives with cherry tomatoes.

- Serve a bunch of chilled Easter egg radishes, with their green tops intact, alongside a ramekin of sea salt for dipping. Have a vessel available for the discarded radish tops.

- For a dramatic look, as a garnish or to eat, carefully shave peeled cucumbers and/or peeled zucchini into long, wide strips using a kitchen mandoline. Place a small amount of both mung bean sprouts and shredded carrots at one end of each strip, then roll up jellyroll fashion and secure with a decorative toothpick/skewer.

- Artichoke hearts, strips of jicama, bite-size pieces of purple cauliflower, cooked yellow beets and raw kohlrabi (both julienne-cut) make up a unique, colorful and nutritious vegetable platter.

- For overall eye-popping appeal, garnish appetizer platters with a single flower atop a leaf or two of fresh greens; Boston/butter/Bibb lettuce leaves work beautifully. My favorite fresh flowers to use as a garnish (not for eating) are Gerber daisies, trimmed of their stems. Their hardy, bright and colorful "faces" sit perfectly flat.

APPETIZERS

Cheese Curry Pâté with Plum Sauce

Baked Brie with Cherry Preserves and Amaretto

Chickpea Mousse with Caramelized Onions

Baked Feta with Roasted Tomatoes and Black Olives

Fried Wontons with Creamy Vegetable Filling

Caviar-Crowned Egg Pâté

Littleneck Clam Dip

Spicy Peanut Chicken

Crab Fritters

Crispy Mushroom Rolls

Guacamole

Honey-Laced Blue Cheese

Hot Queso Texas Dip

Fried Mozzarella Balls

Coconut Peanut Wafers

Savory Pie, Mexican-Style

Tomato and Basil Stuffed Brie

Watch-It-Disappear Horseradish Dip

Baked Bread and Brie with Smashed Grapes

Herbed Cheese with Tapenade and Oven-Roasted Tomatoes

CHEESE CURRY PÂTÉ WITH PLUM SAUCE

This is a mouth-watering combination that always receives rave reviews, even from those who originally said they didn't like curry. For you curry fans out there, this dish is heaven. The flavors in this creation are bold, so it's best to serve with a neutral-flavored cracker. I use McCutcheon's Damson Plum Preserves in this recipe. This recipe yields enough sauce for two to three cheese curry pâtés (depending on the sauce to pâté ratio you prefer) and will keep for several weeks in the refrigerator.

8 ounces light cream cheese, softened
1 cup shredded sharp white cheddar cheese
2 tablespoons cooking sherry
1 teaspoon curry powder
1½ cups plum preserves
1 tablespoon apple cider vinegar
1 tablespoon brown sugar
1 teaspoon red pepper flakes
1 garlic clove, minced
½ teaspoon powdered ginger
thinly sliced green onion (garnish)

In a medium bowl, combine cream cheese, shredded cheddar cheese, sherry and curry powder. Mix until thoroughly combined. Transfer to a serving platter and form mixture into a round shape about 6-inches in diameter. (If you're preparing pâté ahead of time, cover and refrigerate until 30 minutes prior to serving.) In a medium saucepan, combine plum preserves, apple cider vinegar, brown sugar, red pepper flakes, garlic and ginger. Stir mixture until well blended. Bring to a gentle boil, remove from heat and allow the mixture to cool before transferring to a container. Keep at room temperature until ready to use. Just before serving, top pâté with plum sauce and garnish with green onions.

About 25 servings

BAKED BRIE WITH CHERRY PRESERVES AND AMARETTO

I like to use homemade cherry preserves for this recipe, but if you didn't preserve cherries when they were in season, don't skip over this wonderful treat. Instead, use a good quality preserve like Bonne Maman or a brand that has chunky pieces of cherries in it. Serve Brie with crispy, neutral-flavored crackers.

10 ounces Saga Creamy Brie, at room temperature
1 tablespoon amaretto almond liquor
½ cup cherry preserves
⅛ cup sliced almonds

Preheat oven to 350°F. Place Brie in a baking dish large enough to accommodate the cheese. With a sharp knife, slice the top of the cheese as though you were drawing the lines for a game of Tic-Tac-Toe. Drizzle amaretto into cheese "incisions" and cover top with cherry preserves. Sprinkle with sliced almonds. Bake for about 5–10 minutes or until slightly bubbly. Serve immediately.

About 12 servings

CHICKPEA MOUSSE WITH CARAMELIZED ONIONS

This is a nutritious, creamy-textured, delicious spread. Part of what makes it so delicious is tahini: an all-natural, creamy purée made of sesame seeds, which has a light, nut-like flavor. Serve with tortilla chips, pita chips or crispy French bread rounds.

1 can (15 ounces) garbanzo beans (chickpeas), drained
2 garlic cloves
⅓ cup tahini paste
¼ cup olive oil
¼ cup fresh lemon juice
1½ teaspoons salt
¼ teaspoon red pepper flakes
several grindings of freshly ground black pepper
2 tablespoons olive oil
1 large onion, halved and thinly sliced

In a food processor, combine garbanzo beans, garlic, tahini paste, olive oil, lemon juice, salt, red pepper flakes and black pepper. Blend until smooth and creamy. Transfer mixture to a shallow bowl; cover and refrigerate for several hours or overnight. Heat 1 tablespoon olive oil in a large skillet over moderately high heat. Add onions, reduce heat slightly and continue to cook onions, stirring frequently until lightly browned. Allow onions to cool. Just before serving, top mousse with onions and drizzle with remaining tablespoon of olive oil. Serve immediately.

About 8 servings

BAKED FETA WITH ROASTED TOMATOES AND BLACK OLIVES

I like to roast my own tomatoes, I think they taste better homemade, (Oven-Roasted Tomatoes, see page 50). Roast red, yellow, orange or a beautiful assortment of all three types of tomatoes. If you don't roast your own, you can generally find them in the refrigerated section of most major grocery stores. Serve with lightly toasted French bread rounds.

½ pound feta cheese
½ cup roasted red tomatoes in olive oil
½ cup chopped pitted Kalamata olives
¼ teaspoon dried oregano
several grindings of freshly ground black pepper

Preheat oven to 350°F. Cover the bottom of a shallow baking dish with crumbled feta cheese and top with roasted tomatoes. Top tomatoes with olives and sprinkle with oregano and freshly ground black pepper. Bake for 20 minutes. Allow to cool slightly before serving.

About 8 servings

FRIED WONTONS WITH CREAMY VEGETABLE FILLING

This recipe was created the day before we were heading out of town for an extended vacation. We wanted something simple and light to snack on before bedtime since we had enjoyed a heavy bon-voyage lunch with friends earlier in the day. My challenge was to put together something from nearly nothing in our going-on-vacation refrigerator. Nick and I couldn't stop eating these wontons. They are perfect representations of what I'm always looking for in a bite: crispy on the outside and creamy on the inside. The sauce and filling can be prepared in advance, but assemble and sauté the wontons just before serving.

> 12 ounces or 1½ cups mint jelly
> 1 teaspoon red pepper flakes
> 1 teaspoon ground ginger
> 2 garlic cloves, minced
> 8 ounces light cream cheese, softened
> 1 cup finely shredded purple cabbage
> ½ cup thinly sliced green onions
> ¼ teaspoon salt
> 1 package wonton wrappers
> canola oil for frying

In a small saucepan over moderate heat, combine mint jelly, red pepper flakes, ginger and garlic. Bring mixture to a gentle boil and remove from heat. Set aside. In a medium bowl combine cream cheese, shredded cabbage, onions and salt. Place about 1 teaspoon of cream cheese mixture in the center of each wrapper. Fold wonton, corner to corner, forming a triangular shape. (Wonton wrappers are not perfect squares, so when you fold them corner to corner you will not get a perfect triangle.) Dampen finger tips with water and press gently on either side to seal the wontons. Heat canola oil in a large skillet over medium-high heat and cook wontons in batches of 5–7 for about 1–2 minutes on each side or until golden brown and crispy-looking. Place on a paper towel. Transfer to a serving platter and serve immediately along with the mint dipping sauce.

About 48 wontons

CAVIAR-CROWNED EGG PÂTÉ

This dish is beautiful when presented on a rimmed cake platter. Serve with lightly toasted French bread rounds or crispy crackers.

¼ cup (½ stick) butter, softened
⅓ cup finely chopped green onion, plus extra for garnish
¼ cup mayonnaise
½ teaspoon salt (optional)
several grindings of freshly ground black pepper
6 eggs, hard-boiled, minced
¼–½ cup sour cream, enough to cover the pâté
¼ cup red and/or black caviar rinsed, drained and dried

In a large bowl, combine butter, green onions, mayonnaise, salt (if desired) and pepper. Add minced hard-boiled eggs and combine until well blended. Line a 6-inch round container with plastic wrap, allowing enough wrap to overhang the sides. Spoon mixture into container, cover and refrigerate for several hours or overnight. Rinse the caviar under cold running water using a delicate stream; rinse it until the water runs clear. Drain the caviar on paper towels. Place a few paper towels on a rimmed plate and transfer caviar to prepared plate. Cover and refrigerate until serving time.

Plate the pâté for serving by pulling the sides of the wrap from the container and inverting the pâté onto a platter or rimmed cake plate. Spread pâté with sour cream, using the same technique you would use to ice a cake. Just before serving, top pâté with caviar and green onions.

About 12 servings

LITTLENECK CLAM DIP

My clients and friends, The Coopers, requested some clam dishes for a baby clambake they were hosting to welcome their firstborn, Olivia Grace. I created this Littleneck Clam Dip and everyone loved it. Clams come fresh or frozen. If using fresh, you will need to mince about 50–75 clams (depending on their size) to make up 1 cup. Steam them for about 3–5 minutes or until they pop open.

12 ounces whipped cream cheese
8 ounces light cream cheese, softened
1 cup cooked littleneck clams, minced
¼ cup grated onion
2 tablespoons Worcestershire sauce
1 teaspoon dry mustard
1 teaspoon salt

In a large bowl, combine whipped cream cheese, light cream cheese, minced clams, onion, Worcestershire sauce, mustard and salt. Blend until all ingredients are well incorporated. Cover and refrigerate for several hours or overnight. Serve with crispy, fried pita wedges for dipping.

About 15 to 20 servings

Spicy Peanut Chicken

Every time I serve these bite-size morsels, they're devoured within minutes. For a colorful presentation, serve on a bed of shredded carrots. The chicken can be skewered with wooden toothpicks prior to baking, or serve with toothpicks on the side.

¼ cup fresh parsley
¼ cup chopped onion
2 garlic cloves
¼ cup fresh lemon juice
1 tablespoon tamari or soy sauce
1 teaspoon ground coriander
¼ teaspoon cayenne pepper
½ cup natural chunky peanut butter
2 pounds boneless, skinless chicken breast, cut into 1-inch pieces

In a food processor, combine parsley, onion and garlic. Pulse until minced. Add lemon juice, tamari or soy sauce, coriander, cayenne pepper and peanut butter. Process until fully combined; transfer to a large bowl. Add chicken to the marinade and toss (marinade is thick) until well incorporated. Cover and refrigerate for 8 hours.

Preheat oven to 350°F. Arrange chicken in a single layer on a parchment-lined, rimmed baking sheet and bake for about 12 minutes or until chicken is cooked through. Transfer to a serving platter and serve immediately.

About 90 to 100 pieces

CRAB FRITTERS

The first time I served these fritters at a party I was catering, I couldn't fry them fast enough. If you don't have a deep fat fryer, you can use a large skillet that's deep enough for the oil to completely cover the fritters. While they are delicious on their own, they're decadent when dipped in Mustard Cream (see page 37).

2 cups unbleached all-purpose flour
3 teaspoons baking powder
1 teaspoon salt
2 eggs
1 cup heavy cream
¼ cup fresh lemon juice
3 tablespoons minced fresh parsley
1 pound jumbo lump crabmeat, picked of any shell
canola oil for frying

In a large bowl combine flour, baking powder and salt. In a medium bowl, whisk eggs until lightly beaten. Add heavy cream, lemon juice and parsley, and whisk until blended. Add liquid ingredients to the dry ingredients in the large bowl and stir until well combined. Gently fold in crabmeat and refrigerate overnight.

Remove fritter batter about 30 minutes prior to frying. Heat canola oil in a deep fat fryer or a large skillet. When oil is hot, carefully drop batter a scant tablespoonful (or desired amount) at a time into the hot oil. Fry until golden brown. Drain on paper towels and serve immediately.

About 50 fritters

CRISPY MUSHROOM ROLLS

Butter and cream laden rolls: it's no wonder I can't bake these fast enough for guests. The mushroom filling must be prepared the day before assembling the rolls.

4 tablespoons (¼ cup) butter
½ pound fresh mushrooms (about 6–8 medium), finely chopped
3 tablespoons unbleached all-purpose flour
1 cup heavy cream
1 teaspoon salt
½ teaspoon onion powder
1 tablespoon cooking sherry
2 pounds thinly sliced white sandwich bread, crusts removed
2 tablespoons butter

In a medium skillet over moderate heat, melt butter and sauté mushrooms for about 5 minutes. Whisk in flour, 1 tablespoon at a time. Slowly whisk in heavy cream. Add salt, onion powder and sherry, and cook until mixture thickens. Remove from heat and allow the mixture to cool before refrigerating overnight.

Preheat oven to 400°F. Flatten bread slices with a rolling pin, about 12 strokes per slice. Spread a little less than 1 tablespoon mushroom filling evenly over each slice of bread, roll up, and cut each rolled piece in half. Place rolls seam side down on 2 rimmed, parchment-lined baking sheets. Melt butter in a small saucepan; remove from heat and brush rolls with melted butter. Bake for 20–30 minutes (check after 10–15 minutes to ensure even browning; rolls may need to be turned over). Bake until toasty brown. Some of the mushroom mixture seeps out of the rolls while baking. Allow rolls to cool for a minute, and using a knife, tuck the mixture back into its roll. Serve immediately.

About 64 rolls

GUACAMOLE

Guacamole with a surprise ingredient: hard-boiled eggs. The eggs provide added protein and an extra-creamy texture. There are two schools of thought about whether to store the avocado pit with the finished recipe in order to prevent the avocado from changing color. The adding-the-pit school of thought has always worked for me.

> *6 medium, ripe avocados (reserve 1–2 pits)*
> *3 eggs, hard-boiled, finely chopped*
> *⅓ cup grated onion (include whatever juice is produced)*
> *⅓ cup spicy salsa*
> *2 teaspoons salt*

In a large bowl, mash avocados with a fork. Add hard-boiled eggs, onion, salsa and salt; mix until ingredients are fully combined. Add reserved pits and refrigerate until ready to serve. Remove pits just before serving.

About 15 to 20 servings

HONEY-LACED BLUE CHEESE

My cheese of choice is the French Bleu d'Auvergne: mild and moist with tons of blue.

> *½ pound blue cheese wedge, softened*
> *honey*
> *dried fancy pears, Bartlett variety*

Set cheese wedge on a platter. Cover and allow cheese to come to room temperature. Just before serving, drizzle cheese with honey. Serve with dried pears.

About 6 servings

HOT QUESO TEXAS DIP

Every year we were blessed with a visit from our very dear friends from Texas, Beverly Krock and Leonard Humble. While helping them with the menu for a Texas theme party they were hosting, Beverly informed me that a Texas party isn't a Texas party unless you have what "we Texans" call queso dip: melted processed cheese topped with salsa. Below is my unprocessed rendition of this classic, which, by the way, received a Texas thumbs-up from Beverly and Leonard, as well as all of their guests. Serve with guacamole and tortilla chips. Asadero, an off-white, semi-firm Mexican cheese, is great for melting. It can be found in most gourmet cheese departments.

12 ounces Asadero cheese, shredded
1 cup finely chopped onion
1 cup mayonnaise
1 can (4.5 ounces) green chilies, chopped
½ cup mild red salsa

Preheat oven to 350°F. Combine cheese, onion, mayonnaise and green chilies in a 9-inch pie plate. Bake for 30 minutes or until lightly brown. Top with salsa. Serve immediately with tortilla chips.

About 16 servings

Fried Mozzarella Balls

Amazingly simple to prepare and amazingly delicious to eat, these mozzarella balls are yummy on their own, but tomato sauce or salsa make tasty accompaniments. The balls can be prepared in advance and refrigerated. Allow them to come to room temperature before frying.

> *1 pound whole milk mozzarella cheese, cut into chunks*
> *2 eggs*
> *3 tablespoons unbleached all-purpose flour, plus about ½ cup for coating balls*
> *½ cup canola oil*
> *salt (optional)*

Process mozzarella in a food processor until a ball forms. Add eggs and 3 tablespoons of flour; process until fully combined. Place about a ½ cup of flour in a medium bowl. Shape mozzarella mixture into 1-inch balls and roll in flour. In a large skillet, heat canola oil over moderate heat; too high a heat will brown the mozzarella balls too quickly. Fry balls in batches of 10–12 until golden all over. Place on a paper towel, and then transfer to a serving platter. Sprinkle with salt if desired and serve immediately.

About forty 1-inch balls

Coconut Peanut Wafers

This is a unique and tasty wafer. Consider doubling the recipe; guests eat these wafers like peanuts.

½ cup brown rice flour
1 teaspoon coriander
½ teaspoon cumin
¼ teaspoon powdered ginger
1 teaspoon salt
1 cup coconut milk
½ cup chopped roasted, salted peanuts
canola oil for frying

In a medium bowl, combine flour, coriander, cumin, ginger and salt. Add coconut milk and stir until smooth and well blended (batter will be very thin). Stir in peanuts. Cover the bottom of a large skillet with about a ½ inch of canola oil. Heat oil over moderately high heat. Oil should be hot, but not smoking. Drop tablespoons of batter into oil; stand aside—the oil splatters. Batter will spread into a lacy wafer. Cook wafers in small batches (about 2–3 at a time) until golden brown on each side. Transfer to a wire rack. Allow the wafers to cool before eating.

About 15 wafers

SAVORY PIE, MEXICAN-STYLE

I first served this dish to members of the former Baltimore Cooking Club, a club I formed shortly after my first cookbook, *This Book Cooks*, was published. Everyone came back for thirds. The bright, contrasting colors of this savory pie's toppings make a beautiful presentation.

1 cup crushed blue corn tortilla chips
1 tablespoon olive oil
16 ounces light cream cheese, softened
2 eggs
2 cups shredded cheddar cheese
1 package (1¼ ounces) taco seasoning
1 pound lean ground beef
⅓ cup water
1 cup sour cream
1 cup finely chopped yellow pepper
1 cup chopped fresh tomatoes or 1 cup salsa
½ ripe avocado, cut into bite-size pieces

Preheat oven to 325°F. In a 9-inch pie plate, toss crushed tortilla chips with olive oil. Bake for 10 minutes. Remove pie from oven and reset oven temperature to 350°F. In a medium bowl, beat cream cheese until fluffy. Beat in eggs one at a time. Fold in cheddar cheese and 1 teaspoon taco seasoning. Spread cheese mixture evenly over baked tortilla chip crust. In a sauté pan over moderate heat, cook meat until brown. Remove from heat and drain excess fat. Stir in remaining taco seasoning and water, and cook for an additional 2–3 minutes over moderate heat. Cover cheese mixture with meat, and bake at 350°F for 25 minutes. Allow pie to cool for about 10 minutes. Once pie has cooled, spread sour cream evenly over meat, using the same technique you'd use to ice a cake. Top the sour cream with yellow pepper, tomatoes or salsa and avocado, distributing ingredients evenly. Serve immediately with tortilla chips.

About 6 to 8 servings

TOMATO AND BASIL STUFFED BRIE

This recipe is a wonderful choice during the summer, when tomatoes and fresh basil are at the height of their growing season. Serve with Melba toast or French bread rounds that have been brushed with olive oil and baked until lightly toasted. Brie should be split in half (horizontally) when it's cold from the refrigerator. Separate layers with parchment paper and allow them to reach room temperature (about 1–2 hours) prior to assembling.

> *1 tablespoon olive oil*
> *½ cup chopped walnuts*
> *1 cup packed basil leaves, plus extra leaves for garnish*
> *1 cup chopped tomatoes, drained of any juice*
> *salt and freshly ground black pepper, to taste*
> *8 ounces Brie, split in half horizontally*

Heat oil in a sauté pan over moderate heat and sauté walnuts until lightly toasted, about 2–3 minutes. Watch closely so walnuts don't burn. Remove from heat and stir in whole basil leaves and tomatoes; season with salt and pepper. Let mixture cool. Place the bottom half of Brie on a medium rimmed platter. Using a slotted spoon, (you don't want to include any essence from the cooked tomato mixture) spoon half of the tomato/basil mixture over bottom half of Brie. Place the other half of Brie on top and cover with the remaining tomato/basil mixture. Garnish with whole basil leaves. Serve immediately.

About 10 servings

WATCH-IT-DISAPPEAR
HORSERADISH DIP

Every year we visit family in Cleveland, Ohio, and every year they serve what they call "bar dip." It's a zesty, delicious, can't-get-enough dip they buy from a small, independent food store whose long-time owner won't reveal the recipe. I was determined to duplicate this can't-get-enough combination and was very pleased that it only took three attempts to achieve that irresistible, savory flavor. My cousins always serve the dip with crispy bagel chips; I have served it successfully with fresh pineapple chunks, raw vegetables, pretzels and crispy pita chips.

> *8 ounces light whipped cream cheese*
> *1 cup shredded cheddar cheese*
> *¼ cup sour cream*
> *3 tablespoons prepared horseradish*
> *1 vegetable bouillon cube with sea salt, mashed*

In a food processor, combine cream cheese, cheddar cheese, sour cream, horseradish and mashed bouillon cube until well blended, combine making sure that the bouillon cube is fully integrated into mixture. Transfer to a bowl and serve immediately or cover and refrigerate. Serve at room temperature.

About 10 servings

BAKED BREAD AND BRIE WITH SMASHED GRAPES

Had I known this appetizer would be devoured so quickly, I would have doubled the recipe!

2 cups seedless red grapes
5 cups day-old French bread with crust, cut into bite-size cubes
1 pound Brie (after rind has been removed), cut into cubes
¼ cup brown sugar

In a food processor, pulse 1 cup of grapes until minced. Transfer to a small bowl. Rough chop the remaining cup of grapes and toss with minced grapes. Cover and set aside.

Preheat oven to 350°F. Place bread in a 10-inch baking dish that has been coated with cooking spray. Top the bread with cubes of Brie and bake for 15–20 minutes or until lightly browned. Remove from the oven and reset oven temperature to broil. Sprinkle brown sugar over the top of the bread and Brie and place under the broiler for 1–2 minutes or until brown sugar melts. Be careful to not burn the bread. Serve immediately with grapes.

About 8 to 10 servings

HERBED CHEESE WITH TAPENADE AND OVEN-ROASTED TOMATOES

When I was growing up, my parents entertained frequently. My mother would serve a cold and creamy chock-full-of-herbs dip with potato chips, and it was always devoured by her most appreciative guests. The herbed cheese portion of this recipe is a rendition of what she prepared. Serve with crisp, neutral-flavored wafers, crackers or French bread rounds. This recipe makes a large yield, but you can easily cut it in half. Black olive and garlic tapenade can be purchased in the specialty section of most grocery stores. If you don't roast your own tomatoes (Oven-Roasted Tomatoes, see page 50), you can generally find them in most grocery stores.

24 ounces light whipped cream cheese
1 cup finely chopped onion
¼ cup minced fresh parsley
1 teaspoon celery seed
1 teaspoon dried thyme
1 teaspoon salt
1 teaspoon dried oregano
1 teaspoon dried tarragon
1 teaspoon dried basil
several grindings of freshly ground black pepper
1 tablespoon cooking sherry
½ cup black olive and garlic tapenade
½ pound oven-roasted tomatoes, drained of any oil
fresh basil leaves (garnish)

In a large bowl, combine cream cheese with onion, parsley, celery seed, thyme, salt, oregano, tarragon, basil, pepper and sherry. Mix thoroughly. Transfer to a serving platter and form into a round shape about 6-inches in diameter. Cover until ready to serve. Just prior to serving, cover the cheese with black olive tapenade and spoon the oven-roasted tomatoes over the tapenade. Garnish the base of the cheese with fresh basil leaves. Serve immediately.

About 25 to 30 servings

Introducing

ENHANCERS

Thousands of salad dressings, sauces, spreads, marinades, beverages and butters line grocery store shelves. But why not make them from scratch? While many argue that it's far more convenient, less complicated and less time consuming to serve store-bought, I beg to differ. This section is full of really simple, make-in-minutes recipes that should dispel the myth that store-bought is somehow better.

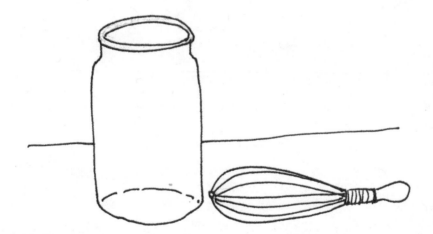

Recipe Overview

ENHANCERS

Salad Dressings

Kerry's All-Purpose Vinaigrette

Basil Walnut Dressing

Tarragon Dressing

Fresh-Squeezed Orange Dressing

Apple Cider Celery Seed Dressing

Creams and Sauces

Tomato Cinnamon Clove Cream

Make-in-Minutes Chocolate Sauce

Horseradish Cream

Mustard Cream

Raspberry Orange Cranberry Sauce

Pumpkin Cream

Red Curry Sauce

Gingered Rhubarb Sauce

Beverages

Fruité Maté Smoothé

Hibiscus Tea over Candied Ginger Ice

Seasonal Sangria

Miscellaneous

Better Butter

Autumn Orange Butter

User-Friendly Pie Crust

Apricot Ginger Cream Cheese Spread

Teriyaki Marinade

Oven-Roasted Tomatoes

Roasted In-Season Vegetables

Salad Dressings

KERRY'S ALL-PURPOSE VINAIGRETTE

This is an all-purpose dressing that is so delicious and can be prepared so quickly, you might ask yourself why you ever bought bottled vinaigrette. Vinaigrette will keep for several days in the refrigerator. Allow to come to room temperature before serving.

> *¼ cup apple cider vinegar*
> *1 teaspoon salt*
> *several grindings of freshly ground black pepper*
> *1 teaspoon Dijon-style mustard*
> *¾ cup extra virgin olive oil*

In a 2-cup jar with a tight-fitting lid, combine apple cider vinegar, salt, pepper, and mustard. Shake until ingredients are well blended and salt has dissolved. Add olive oil and shake again to combine ingredients. Store at room temperature until ready to serve. Shake well just prior to using. Refrigerate any unused portion.

About 1 cup

BASIL WALNUT DRESSING

When basil is at the peak of its growing season, this is the perfect dressing to pour over slices of ripe summer tomatoes or toss with your favorite pasta.

> ¼ cup apple cider vinegar
> 1 teaspoon salt
> several grindings of freshly ground black pepper
> 1 teaspoon Dijon-style mustard
> ¾ cup olive oil
> 1 cup fresh basil leaves
> ½ cup walnuts

In a food processor, combine vinegar, salt, pepper, and mustard; whirl until well blended. With the motor running, slowly pour olive oil through the feed tube; process until dressing is emulsified. Add basil leaves and walnuts, and pulse mixture until walnuts are finely chopped. If you won't be using the dressing immediately, transfer to a 2-cup jar with tight-fitting lid and refrigerate. Allow to come to room temperature before serving. Shake just prior to using.

About 1½ cups

TARRAGON DRESSING

I tossed my Leafy Greens with Radish and Eggs (see page 173) with this delicious Tarragon Dressing and served it to members of my cooking club. The combination received rave reviews. This dressing also makes a great marinade for chicken. As with most oil and vinegar dressings, this can be prepared in advance and keeps for several days in the refrigerator. Allow the dressing to come to room temperature before serving.

> ¼ cup apple cider vinegar
> 1 teaspoon salt
> several grindings of freshly ground black pepper
> 1 teaspoon Dijon-style mustard
> ¾ cup extra virgin olive oil
> 1 teaspoon dried tarragon

In a 2-cup jar with a tight-fitting lid, combine apple cider vinegar, salt and pepper. Shake contents until well combined. Add mustard and olive oil, and shake contents until incorporated; add tarragon. Store at room temperature until ready to serve; shake just prior to using.

About 1 cup

FRESH-SQUEEZED ORANGE DRESSING

Fresh-Squeezed Orange Dressing will keep for several days in the refrigerator. Bring to room temperature before serving.

1 teaspoon salt
several grindings of freshly ground black pepper
1 teaspoon Dijon-style mustard
¼ cup orange juice, freshly squeezed
¾ cup canola oil

In a 2-cup jar with a tight-fitting lid, combine salt, black pepper, mustard and orange juice. Add canola oil ¼ cup at a time, shaking well after each addition. Keep dressing at room temperature until ready to serve. Shake just before using. Refrigerate any unused portion.

About 1 cup

APPLE CIDER CELERY SEED DRESSING

This crowd-pleasing dressing is delicious tossed with any combination of salad ingredients and raw vegetables. It also enhances cold pasta dishes and fresh fruit.

> *⅓ cup sugar*
> *1 teaspoon salt*
> *1 teaspoon dry mustard*
> *1 teaspoon freshly minced onion*
> *¼ cup apple cider vinegar*
> *1 cup canola oil*
> *1 teaspoon celery seeds*

In a medium bowl, combine sugar, salt and dry mustard. Add onion and apple cider vinegar. Slowly add oil, whisking constantly. You'll see the mixture change texture as you whisk. After all the oil has been added and dressing has thickened, stir in celery seeds. Mix until well blended. Transfer dressing to a 2-cup jar with a tight-fitting lid and refrigerate. (Apple Cider Celery Seed Dressing will last for several days in the refrigerator.) Allow to come to room temperature before serving. Shake well prior to using.

About 1½ cups

Creams and Sauces

TOMATO CINNAMON CLOVE CREAM

This unusual and flavorful cream was created for a cocktail party that Nick and I hosted. I slathered it on homemade Focaccia (see page 220) and topped the cream with thin slices of marinated beef tenderloin. The results were outstanding, and the open-faced sandwiches were devoured within minutes. For cream to properly whip, place the bowl and/or the beaters in the freezer for several hours prior to preparing the whip cream. Tomato Cinnamon Clove Preserves is one of many wonderful food products created by A Perfect Pear from Napa Valley. You can also experiment with similar tomato preserve products found in farmers markets. This delicious cream is best prepared just before serving.

> *1 cup heavy whipping cream*
> *¼ cup A Perfect Pear Tomato Cinnamon Clove Preserves*
> *2 tablespoons Dijon-style mustard*
> *1 tablespoon Worcestershire sauce*
> *1 tablespoon mayonnaise*

In a medium bowl, whip cream until slightly stiff. Watch carefully: if you over-whip the cream, it will turn to butter. Fold in preserves, mustard, Worcestershire sauce and mayonnaise. Serve immediately or refrigerate until ready to serve.

About 2½ cups

MAKE-IN-MINUTES CHOCOLATE SAUCE

This chocolate sauce recipe from my grandmother is delicious and simple to prepare. The first time I served it, my husband and I were hosting a small party in Gibson Island, Maryland. It was a warm June evening, and as we watched the sun lose itself to the horizon, we ate chocolate dipped strawberries with gay abandon. I use the same brand of condensed milk my grandmother used, Borden Eagle Brand Sweetened Condensed Milk.

2 ounces semi-sweet chocolate
1 can (14 ounces) sweetened condensed milk, regular
1 teaspoon vanilla

In a medium saucepan over low heat, melt chocolate. Add condensed milk and stir mixture until well blended. Add vanilla, and stir well; remove from heat. Serve at room temperature.

About 1½ cups

HORSERADISH CREAM

This cream is an excellent complement to salmon or beef. For cream to properly whip, place the bowl and/or the beaters in the freezer for several hours prior to preparing the whip cream. Horseradish Cream is best prepared just before serving.

½ cup heavy whipping cream
⅓ cup prepared horseradish
1 tablespoon Dijon-style mustard
2 teaspoons Worcestershire sauce
½ teaspoon salt

In a medium bowl, beat whipping cream on medium speed. When the cream thickens, increase the speed and continue to beat until cream falls in large globs and has soft peaks. Fold in horseradish, mustard, Worcestershire sauce and salt; combine until well blended. Serve immediately, or refrigerate until ready to serve.

About 1½ cups

MUSTARD CREAM

This is one of those recipes that you'll keep coming back to again and again. Mustard Cream always generates a "wow" response, whether you're dipping Crab Fritters in it (see page 12) or serving it alongside beef, chicken or pork. For cream to properly whip, place the bowl and/or the beaters in the freezer for several hours prior to preparing the whip cream. Mustard Cream is best when whipped up just before serving.

> *1 cup heavy whipping cream*
> *⅓ cup Dijon-style mustard*
> *1 tablespoon Worcestershire sauce*

Pour whipping cream into medium bowl and beat on medium speed. When the cream thickens, increase the speed and continue to beat until cream falls in large globs and has soft peaks. Fold in mustard and Worcestershire sauce. Serve immediately, or refrigerate until ready to serve.

About 2½ cups

RASPBERRY ORANGE CRANBERRY SAUCE

Cranberries have a distinctively tart flavor; for some, too tart. In this recipe, I've offset the tartness by adding sugar, cranberry-raspberry juice and orange marmalade. The result is a delicious sauce that is a complementary companion to chicken, pork and various cheeses. Nick and I use it as a spread on turkey sandwiches and have even spooned it over vanilla yogurt for a light dessert. This recipe takes minutes to prepare, can be made in advance and will keep for several weeks refrigerated.

12 ounces fresh cranberries, rinsed
1 cup sugar
1 cup cranberry-raspberry juice
¼ cup orange marmalade

In a medium saucepan over medium-high heat, combine cranberries, sugar, cranberry-raspberry juice and orange marmalade. Bring to a boil, reduce heat and cook mixture until berries pop open, about 8–10 minutes. Allow sauce to cool before serving.

About 2½ cups

Pumpkin Cream

Pumpkin Pie in a Jar (apple pumpkin butter) from La Provençale Cellars, is a combination of all the flavors you adore in a traditional pumpkin pie. I first came across this product when I was writing my column, New Bites, for *Smart Woman* magazine, and as with all new discoveries, I couldn't wait to come up with my own use for it. I developed Pumpkin Cream for an October issue, and just before publication, invited friends over to sample it. Sesame Pork Tenderloin (*This Book Cooks*) was topped with Pumpkin Cream as a substitute for Mustard Cream (see page 37). Everyone loved the combination.

For cream to properly whip, place the bowl and/or the beaters in the freezer for several hours prior to preparing the whip cream. For best results, assemble Pumpkin Cream just prior to serving. Pumpkin Pie in a Jar can be ordered online from www.lemousseux.com. If you're not inclined to order online, apple butter can be used with nearly the same results.

½ cup heavy whipping cream
½ cup Pumpkin Pie in a Jar or apple butter

Pour heavy cream into a medium bowl and beat on medium-high speed. When cream thickens, increase speed and continue to beat until soft peaks form. Fold in Pumpkin Pie in a Jar or apple butter. Serve immediately, or refrigerate until just before serving.

About 1½ cups

RED CURRY SAUCE

This zesty, simple-to-prepare dipping sauce is delicious served with chicken, fish or tofu, or spoon over your favorite grain. Red curry paste is a spicy, concentrated, seasoned mixture of fresh red chilies and Thai spices. It can be found in the international aisle of most grocery stores. Red Curry Sauce can be prepared in advance and will keep for a few days if refrigerated.

> *½ cup tamari or soy sauce*
> *2 tablespoons water*
> *1 tablespoon toasted sesame oil*
> *1 tablespoon sliced green onions*
> *1 teaspoon red curry paste*

In a medium bowl, using a wire whisk, combine tamari or soy sauce, water, sesame oil, green onions and red curry paste. Whisk until well blended.

About ⅔ cup

GINGERED RHUBARB SAUCE

In May 2008, the Baltimore chapter of Slow Food USA launched our Eat In-Season Restaurant Challenge. As the innovator of this challenge, as well as the Chair of the Challenge Committee, I hosted a breakfast to introduce the concept to the press. My self-appointed challenge was to come up with a menu using foods that were in-season in Maryland during the month of May. Rhubarb was the only available local food in season that seemed appropriate; thus, it became the focus of this Gingered Rhubarb Sauce and the Rhubarb Cake (see page 250). The press breakfast was such a success that Rob Kasper, the food editor for our local newspaper, *The Sun*, wrote an article about the Restaurant Challenge that included both recipes.

Gingered Rhubarb Sauce is delicious spooned over strawberry ice cream or vanilla yogurt. For an unusual breakfast idea, serve rhubarb parfaits like I served to the press; fill tulip-shaped glasses with vanilla yogurt, and top with rhubarb sauce and granola. This versatile sauce can also be served as a condiment (just as you would applesauce) with grilled chicken, pork and crispy duck.

> *4 cups sliced (¼-inch thick) rhubarb*
> *½ cup water*
> *½ cup sugar*
> *¼ teaspoon powdered ginger*

Place rhubarb and water in a medium saucepan. The ratio of water to rhubarb may seem disproportionate, but too much water will result in a watery sauce. Over moderate heat, cook rhubarb for about 15–20 minutes or until tender. Stir every 5–10 minutes. Remove from heat and stir in sugar and ginger. Serve warm or at room temperature.

About 4 cups

Beverages

FRUITÉ MATÉ SMOOTHÉ

A smoothie is generally defined as a blended, chilled beverage made from fresh or frozen fruit or vegetables pureed with yogurt or milk. Honey, agave nectar, protein powders, nutritional supplements and a variety of teas can also be added. To boost antioxidant levels, I've included Pixie Maté; for every four ounces of liquid concentrate you add to a smoothie, you're packing about five times the antioxidants of a serving of green tea.

You can experiment with all sorts of combinations of seasonal fruits. Pixie Maté, The Original Maté Latte concentrate is available from most health-oriented grocery stores.

> *1 ripe banana*
> *1 peach, fresh or frozen*
> *½ cup fresh pitted cherries (or frozen)*
> *½ cup Pixie Maté*

Place ingredients in a blender. Blend until smooth and creamy. Serve immediately.

About 16 ounces

HIBISCUS TEA OVER CANDIED GINGER ICE

The brilliant crimson-colored hibiscus tea leaves turn out a beautiful glass of iced tea. This recipe further enhances the tea's mild citrus flavor; cold tea is poured over ginger-infused ice cubes. It's a refreshing and zesty drink for summer sipping, for entertaining, or just to have on hand. Prepare the ice cubes the day before you plan to serve the tea. My preferred method of steeping tea is in cold water. It's faster—no boiling water or waiting for tea to cool. Candied ginger can be found in most major health-oriented grocery stores.

> ¼ cup crystallized (candied) ginger
> 1 family-size Hibiscus Tea bag
> fresh mint (garnish)

Finely chop approximately ¼ cup candied ginger and place a few pieces of ginger into each compartment of 2 ice cube trays. Fill trays with water and freeze overnight. Place tea bag in a large pitcher (at least 2-quart capacity) and fill with cold water. Steep for 15–20 minutes in the refrigerator; the longer the better. Garnish each glass with a fresh sprig of mint or a mint leaf.

Eight 8-ounce glasses

Seasonal Sangria

Warm summer nights call for a refreshing beverage like Summer Sangria: chilled white wine combined with colorful summer fruit. Colder months typically call for heavier red wines and the fruits that represent those seasons. Here are recipes for both summer and winter versions. Sangria is a great beverage to serve when you are hosting and you don't want to spend time preparing drinks or when you want to limit your beverage choices to one or two items. Plan ahead. The first four ingredients get combined the day before you plan to serve the sangria. Fruit should be ripe but firm.

Summer Sangria

1 bottle (750ml) white wine
½ cup triple sec or Cointreau
½ cup brandy
¼ cup sugar
1 bottle (750ml) sparkling wine or champagne, chilled
¼ cup or more per serving, any combination of: honeydew, cantaloupe, peaches, pitted cherries and strawberries, cut into bite-size pieces, whole blueberries, raspberries and blackberries

Winter Sangria

1 bottle (750ml) red wine
½ cup triple sec or Cointreau
½ cup brandy
¼ cup sugar
1 bottle (750ml) sparkling wine or champagne, chilled
¼ cup or more per serving, any combination of: pineapple, pears and apples, cut into bite-size pieces and orange segments

In a 2-quart container, combine wine, triple sec or Cointreau, brandy and sugar. Refrigerate overnight. Just before serving, add chilled sparkling wine or champagne to wine mixture; and stir to blend. Place fruit into a large punch bowl or divide equally into two 2-quart pitchers. I prefer using clear glass containers as this is such a beautiful beverage. Pour or ladle sangria over fruit.

About 4 to 6 servings

Miscellaneous

BETTER BUTTER

When you combine equal amounts of butter and oil, you get the flavor of butter with only half the saturated fat and cholesterol. If you prefer a savory, robust-tasting butter, use olive oil in this recipe; for an all-purpose flavor, combine butter with canola oil.

½ cup (1 stick) butter, softened
½ cup olive or canola oil

Blend butter and oil in a medium bowl, using a wire whisk or a mixer, until fully incorporated. Transfer to a container and refrigerate for several hours (or until firm) before serving.

About 1 cup

Autumn Orange Butter

I've combined butter and orange juice with The Spice Hunter Winter Sippers Hot Buttered Rum Mix, a complementary blend of brown sugar, cinnamon, nutmeg, cardamom, allspice, cloves and lemon oil. Spiced Orange Butter is wonderful slathered on Hot-Buttered-Rum Pumpkin Biscuits (see page 216) as well as on pancakes and waffles. Winter Sippers Hot Buttered Rum Mix is available from Whole Foods Market and many specialty grocery stores during the Thanksgiving and Christmas holiday seasons.

½ cup (1 stick) butter, softened
1 tablespoon orange juice
1 tablespoon Winter Sippers Hot Buttered Rum Mix

In a medium bowl, combine butter, orange juice and Winter Sippers Hot Buttered Rum Mix. Whisk until fully combined. Refrigerate for several hours, or until firm, before serving.

About ½ cup

USER-FRIENDLY PIE CRUST

Surprisingly, oil replaces the shortening usually found in pie crust recipes, making this crust a heart-healthier alternative. Once you see how easy it is to prepare a pie crust, you might not ever go back to using store-bought. The dough can be prepared in advance and refrigerated until ready to use. Allow it to come to room temperature before rolling.

> *1⅛ cups unbleached all-purpose flour*
> *½ teaspoon salt*
> *¼ cup canola oil*
> *2½ tablespoons cold water*

In a large bowl, combine flour and salt. Pour oil over flour and toss until mixture is coarse. Add cold water. Using your hands, bring flour mixture together until ingredients are fully incorporated. Add more water (a little at a time) if the dough doesn't come together or seems dry. Let dough rest for about 5 minutes. Preheat oven to 425°F. Lightly flour a work surface and roll dough (if dough begins to resist, let it stand for about 5 minutes) into a 12-inch circle. Transfer dough to a 9-inch pie plate and flute the edges using the dough that overlaps the pie plate. Prick the shell with a fork in several places to ensure even baking. Bake for 12–15 minutes or until light brown.

One 9-inch pie crust

APRICOT GINGER CREAM CHEESE SPREAD

I've combined crystallized (candied) ginger for texture and powdered ginger for its concentrated flavor. The result is a zesty spread that is simple to assemble. Nick and I love to spread it on plain bagels.

8 ounces light cream cheese, softened
⅓ cup apricot preserves
1½ tablespoons finely chopped crystallized ginger
½ teaspoon powdered ginger

In a medium bowl, combine cream cheese, apricot preserves, crystallized and powdered ginger. Mix until well blended. Serve immediately or refrigerate until 30 minutes prior to use.

About 1½ cups

TERIYAKI MARINADE

This is an easy-to-make marinade that makes a wonderful, flavorful dish with whatever you're marinating—chicken, beef or pork. One cup of marinade is generally enough for 1–2 pounds of meat.

> ½ cup tamari or soy sauce
> ¼ cup canola oil
> 1 tablespoon cooking sherry
> 1 tablespoon brown sugar
> 2 garlic cloves, mashed
> ½ teaspoon powdered ginger

In the container you're going to use for marinating, combine tamari or soy sauce, canola oil, sherry, brown sugar, garlic and ginger. Whisk until combined. Add chicken, beef or pork and marinate in refrigerator. Turn a couple of times during marinating process. After marinating, discard used marinade.

About 1 cup

OVEN-ROASTED TOMATOES

I love to roast tomatoes when they're at the peak of their growing season. Roast red, yellow or orange tomatoes for the same taste results; roast a combination of colors for a beautiful presentation. Cooking tomatoes for a long time will shrink them to about half their original amount.

> *4 medium tomatoes, sliced*
> *olive oil*
> *coarse salt*

Preheat oven to 400°F. Arrange tomatoes in a single layer on a rimmed baking sheet. Drizzle with olive oil and season with salt. Roast tomatoes for 30–40 minutes or until slightly blackened. Serve at room temperature.

About ½ to 1 cup

ROASTED IN-SEASON VEGETABLES

I find myself roasting vegetables often, from the end of summer through early fall. I especially like the wonderful, sweet flavor that results from the roasting method—the long cooking time in a hot oven caramelizes the vegetables and blackens them slightly. Any color pepper works: red, yellow, green, orange or try one of each. Cooking vegetables for a long time will shrink them to about half their original amount. When refrigerated, the vegetables will keep for about a week.

4 peppers, cut into 1 x 1-inch chunks
4 medium tomatoes, cut into chunks
4 medium onions, cut into 1 x 1-inch chunks
4 large carrots or parsnips, peeled, cut ¼-inch thick, then julienne-sliced
olive oil
coarse salt

Preheat oven to 400°F. In a large bowl, combine peppers, tomatoes, onions and carrots or parsnips. Toss vegetables with olive oil and season with salt. Transfer vegetables onto 2 rimmed baking sheets; give each pan a light shake to evenly distribute. Roast the vegetables for about 1½–2 hours or until slightly blackened. For even roasting, shift baking sheets and stir vegetables every ½ hour. Serve at room temperature.

About 4 cups

BREAKFAST AND BRUNCH

Inside the Breakfast and Brunch section, you'll find a unique collection of morning and midday recipes that have remained long-time favorites among my family and friends. Many can be prepared in advance (some the day before)—a feature that's very important when entertaining, especially when hosting an event early in the day.

Many of the pancake, waffle and muffin recipes include diverse and nutrient-rich ingredients like Salba, wheat germ, teff, flax seeds and buckwheat. Fruits and vegetables like plums, peaches, pumpkin and parsnips are incorporated for extra color, flavor and fiber.

Eggs take center stage in various quiche recipes, like Vegan Sausage and Spinach Quiche as well as Oven-Roasted Tomato Quiche. And if you're looking to make a great impression plus feel proud of your endeavor, make sure to prepare Puffed Savory Egg Strudel. On top of the great recipes found in this section, you'll also learn a new and unique method of cooking eggs called froaching, Froached Eggs over Seasoned Fresh Greens.

French toast is prepared two different ways: French Toasted Croissants with Blueberry Sauce, which replaces traditional bread with croissants, and Lemon Cardamom French Toast Sandwiches. And then there are irresistibly aromatic breakfast cakes like Cherry Almond Coffee Cake and Mango and Cardamom Coffee Cake with Almond Streusel.

BREAKFAST AND BRUNCH

Cherry Almond Coffeecake

Powerhouse Blueberry Waffles

Puffed Savory Egg Strudel

Lemon Cardamom French Toast Sandwiches

Spinach and Mushroom Quiche

Cranberry Walnut Muffins

Froached Eggs over Seasoned Fresh Greens

Hot-Buttered-Rum Pumpkin Pancakes

Chestnut Cherry Waffles

Maté Chai Latte Muffins

Plum Perfect Pancakes

Oven-Roasted Tomato Quiche

Nutrient-Rich Breakfast Muffins

Crunchy Banana Waffles

Peach Pancakes

Naturally-Sweetened Blueberry Muffins

French-Toasted Croissants with Blueberry Sauce

Mango and Cardamom Coffee Cake with Almond Streusel

Buckwheat Parsnip Waffles

Vegan Sausage and Spinach Quiche

Chestnut Pancakes

CHERRY ALMOND COFFEE CAKE

The addition of fresh cherries makes this breakfast, brunch and dessert cake incredibly moist, and the perfect foundation for the crunchy almond, brown sugar, cinnamon topping. Like most coffee cakes, this tastes best eaten hot from the oven. Spreading it with butter is an option I enthusiastically endorse. Cherry season is sweet but notoriously short, so make sure it doesn't slip away before you can sample this delicious coffee cake.

1 cup unbleached all-purpose flour
½ cup sugar
1 teaspoon baking powder
½ teaspoon salt
¼ teaspoon baking soda
1 cup pitted, rough chopped fresh sweet cherries
⅔ cup almond milk
2 tablespoons canola oil
½ teaspoon almond extract
1 egg
⅓ cup sliced almonds
1 tablespoon brown sugar
¼ teaspoon cinnamon
butter (optional)

Preheat oven to 350°F. Coat an 8-inch square baking pan with cooking spray. In a large bowl, combine flour, sugar, baking powder, salt and baking soda. Toss flour mixture with ½ cup cherries. In a medium bowl, combine almond milk, canola oil, almond extract and egg and whisk until well blended. Pour liquid mixture into flour/cherry mixture and stir until well incorporated. Transfer batter into prepared baking pan and top with remaining ½ cup cherries. In a small bowl, combine almonds, brown sugar and cinnamon. Sprinkle over coffee cake batter. Bake for 35 minutes or until a toothpick inserted in center comes out clean. Serve immediately. Top with butter if desired.

6 servings

POWERHOUSE BLUEBERRY WAFFLES

When these little nutrient powerhouses are in season, I often prepare these tasty and wholesome waffles for breakfast. The addition of flax seeds and Salba in this recipe enhances the nutritional value of the waffles, as well as adding a welcome crunch. I prefer to use whole flax seeds and whole seed Salba and grind them just prior to use. A coffee grinder works perfectly for this.

1 cup unbleached all-purpose flour
¼ cup whole flax seeds, ground
¼ cup whole seed Salba, ground
¼ cup yellow cornmeal
2 teaspoons baking powder
½ teaspoon salt
3 eggs, separated
½ cup canola oil
1½ cups milk
1 cup rough chopped fresh blueberries
butter and syrup

Prepare waffle iron according to directions. In a large bowl, combine flour, ground flax seeds, ground Salba, cornmeal, baking powder and salt. In a medium bowl, whisk egg yolks with oil and milk. Make a well in the center of the dry ingredients and pour in liquid ingredients. Combine with a few swift strokes. Gently fold in blueberries. In a medium bowl, beat egg whites until stiff. Fold into batter, just barely blending. When waffle iron is ready, spoon a heaping ½ cup of the batter into the center of the waffle iron. Cook until light brown or until waffle iron indicator light goes out. Serve immediately with butter and syrup.

5 waffles

PUFFED SAVORY EGG STRUDEL

Have you ever pulled something from the oven and been wowed by the results? That's exactly what happened to me the first time I prepared this savory strudel. Puff pastry needs to thaw before it's ready to roll. Not every brand has the same thawing directions; check the package ahead of time. I do not recommend preparing this dish in advance.

2 sheets puff pastry dough
12 eggs
¼ cup milk
½ cup shredded carrots
½ cup chopped onions
½ cup chopped red pepper
1 teaspoon salt
several grindings of freshly ground black pepper
2 tablespoons olive oil
1 cup shredded Swiss cheese

Preheat oven to 400°F. Line two rimmed baking sheets with parchment paper. Lightly coat a work surface with flour. Unfold pastry sheets; roll each sheet into a 12 x 12-inch square, and transfer each to a baking sheet. With a sharp knife, cut diagonal strips (about a 45° angle) down both sides of each pastry sheet; cuts should be about 4 inches in length, and each strip of dough should be about 1 inch wide. In a large bowl, whisk eggs with milk. Add carrots, onions, red pepper, salt and pepper. Heat olive oil in a large skillet over moderate heat. Add egg mixture and scramble until just set. (Remember, eggs are going to be baked.) Spoon half of the eggs down the center of each prepared pastry sheet; diagonal cuts will be on both sides of the eggs. Working either down from the top of the pastry sheet or up from the bottom, cross over the filling with the strips of dough, alternating strips. This process does not have to be perfect; the pastry puffs up during baking, covering any imperfections. Brush top of pastry with water and sprinkle each strudel with ½ cup of shredded cheese. Bake for 25 minutes or until golden brown. Allow strudel to cool for about 5 minutes before serving.

8 to 10 servings

LEMON CARDAMOM FRENCH TOAST SANDWICHES

I love to serve this delicious and unusual dish when we're entertaining another couple for breakfast or brunch. Not only is it impressive, I especially like that it must be prepared in advance. Then I have more time to spend with my friends. Pork sausage, vegetarian sausage or bacon plus seasonal fruits are wonderful accompaniments.

4 ounces light whipped cream cheese
1 teaspoon cardamom
2 teaspoons finely grated lemon peel
1 tablespoon fresh lemon juice
8 slices (½-inch) Tuscan bread
4 eggs
½ cup half-and-half
1–2 tablespoons canola oil
butter and syrup

In a small bowl, combine cream cheese, cardamom, lemon peel, and lemon juice. Spread cream cheese mixture evenly over four slices of bread; top each slice with second slice of bread. Whisk eggs with half-and-half in a baking dish that will accommodate 4 sandwiches in a single layer. Place sandwiches in egg mixture and allow them to soak for about 5 minutes on each side. Refrigerate sandwiches overnight.

Allow sandwiches to come to room temperature (about 30 minutes). Heat canola oil in a large skillet over moderately high heat, and cook sandwiches (in batches of 2 or in two skillets) until golden brown on each side. Serve immediately with butter and syrup.

4 servings

SPINACH AND MUSHROOM QUICHE

This complete meal takes a little time to put together (mainly because of the homemade crust), but the time is more than worth it.

If you're short on time, a store-bought crust will work.

> *1⅛ cups all-purpose flour*
> *½ teaspoon salt*
> *¼ cup olive oil*
> *2½–3 tablespoons cold water*

In a medium bowl, combine flour and salt. Drizzle olive oil over flour and toss until flour mixture is coarse. Slowly drizzle in cold water; add more water if dough doesn't come together or seems dry. Knead dough a few times to fully incorporate ingredients. Let dough rest for about 5 minutes. Lightly flour work surface and roll dough (if dough begins to resist, let it rest for about 5 minutes) until it's about 12 inches in diameter. Transfer to a 9-inch pie plate. Flute edges.

> *1 tablespoon olive oil*
> *1 cup finely chopped onion*
> *½ pound finely chopped mushrooms (about 6 medium)*
> *8 eggs*
> *½ cup half-and-half*
> *½ teaspoon salt*
> *a dash cayenne pepper*
> *3 cups shredded cheddar cheese*
> *16 ounces frozen chopped spinach, defrosted, drained, and squeezed dry*

Preheat oven to 350°F. Heat olive oil in a medium sauté pan over moderate heat. Add onion and mushrooms, and cook until mushrooms are soft. In a large bowl, whisk eggs with half-and-half, salt and cayenne pepper. Sprinkle 1 cup of cheese in the bottom of unbaked pie crust. Top the cheese with ½ of the spinach and ½ of the mushroom mixture. Top with 1 cup cheese. Top with remaining spinach and remaining mushroom mixture. Pour egg mixture evenly over the spinach/mushroom mixture, and top with remaining cheese. Bake for 45 minutes. Allow pie to sit for 10 minutes before serving.

6 servings

CRANBERRY WALNUT MUFFINS

I like to serve these muffins when the weather has turned cooler. To toast millet, bake in a 350°F oven or toaster oven until lightly browned. Watch closely: millet toasts very quickly.

1 cup unbleached all-purpose flour
⅓ cup cornmeal
⅓ cup teff flour
⅓ cup brown sugar
¼ cup millet, toasted
1 teaspoon salt
1 teaspoon baking soda
2 eggs
¾ cup plain yogurt
⅓ cup canola oil
1 teaspoon vanilla
1 cup chopped walnuts
1 cup dried cranberries

Preheat oven to 350°F. Generously oil a 12-capacity muffin tin with cooking spray. In a large bowl, combine flour, cornmeal, teff flour, brown sugar, toasted millet, salt and baking soda. In a medium bowl, lightly beat eggs, and add yogurt, canola oil and vanilla and stir until well blended. Add to flour mixture and combine ingredients until well incorporated. Gently fold in walnuts and cranberries. Distribute evenly into muffin tin and bake for 12–15 minutes or until toothpick inserted into center of a muffin comes out clean. Cool for about 5–10 minutes before removing muffins from the tin.

12 muffins

Froached Eggs over Seasoned Fresh Greens

My first experience with a "froached" egg was at a Bed and Breakfast in Scotland. Our hostess explained the cooking method as a wee bit fried and a wee bit poached. Start out as though you're simply frying the eggs in oil, but as soon as the bottoms are firm (about thirty seconds), add a wee bit of water to the skillet and cover with a tight-fitting lid. This creates the steaming method used to poach eggs. In this recipe, warm and wonderful froached eggs pair beautifully with delicate and perfectly seasoned lettuce leaves. Roasted sunflower seeds and sprouts give this dynamic-tasting combination great texture.

Kerry's All-Purpose Vinaigrette (see page 29)

This vinaigrette recipe yields more than you'll need for this dish.
Keep dressing at room temperature until ready to use. Refrigerate any unused portion.

> *4 generous handfuls lettuce leaves, torn into bite-size pieces*
> *1–2 tablespoons canola oil*
> *4 eggs*
> *salt and pepper, to taste*
> *⅓–½ cup water*
> *roasted and salted sunflower seeds, a scant tablespoon per person*
> *sprouts (garnish)*

In a large bowl, toss salad greens with the vinaigrette; just enough to coat the leaves. Divide salad greens among four shallow serving bowls. Heat canola oil in a large skillet over medium heat. Add eggs one at a time, and season with salt and pepper to taste. Add just enough water to cover the bottom of the pan; put a lid on the skillet, and cook for about 1 minute or until white is firm and yolk is soft. Top salad greens with a froached egg, sunflower seeds and desired amount of sprouts. Serve immediately.

4 servings

Hot-Buttered-Rum Pumpkin Pancakes

The Spice Hunter Winter Sippers Hot Buttered Rum Mix is a blend of brown sugar, cinnamon, nutmeg, cardamom, allspice, cloves and lemon oil. This harmonious medley of ingredients is what gives these pancakes their distinctive flavor. Be sure to use real pumpkin and not pumpkin pie filling. You can use the extra pumpkin in the Pumpkin Roll-Up Cake with Cream Cheese Filling (see page 237).

> *1½ cups unbleached all-purpose flour*
> *3 tablespoons Winter Sippers Hot Buttered Rum Mix*
> *1½ teaspoons baking powder*
> *½ teaspoon baking soda*
> *½ teaspoon salt*
> *2 eggs*
> *1 cup milk*
> *1 cup canned pumpkin*
> *2 tablespoons canola oil*
> *1 teaspoon vanilla*
> *butter and syrup*

In a large bowl, combine flour, Winter Sippers Hot Buttered Rum Mix, baking powder, baking soda and salt. In a medium bowl, whisk eggs, milk, pumpkin, canola oil and vanilla until fully combined. Pour liquid mixture into flour mixture, stirring just to combine. In a large skillet, heat about 1 tablespoon canola oil over moderate heat. Spoon or pour about ¼ cup batter per pancake into skillet; a large skillet should cook approximately 3 at a time. Cook pancakes for 1–2 minutes per side or until golden brown. Serve immediately with butter and syrup.

14 to 16 pancakes

CHESTNUT CHERRY WAFFLES

We were looking at a ninety percent chance of snow, but we didn't care. What better way to spend a raw Sunday morning than curled up in front of a roaring fire, reading the newspaper, sipping good coffee and eating these delicious, garnet-speckled waffles? Let it snow. Let it snow. Let it snow!

> *1½ cups unbleached all-purpose flour*
> *½ cup chestnut flour*
> *2 teaspoons baking powder*
> *½ teaspoon salt*
> *2 eggs, separated*
> *1 cup milk*
> *⅓ cup canola oil*
> *1 can (15 ounces) Bing cherries, drained, coarsely chopped*
> *1 teaspoon vanilla*
> *butter and syrup*

Prepare waffle iron according to directions. In a large bowl, combine flour, chestnut flour, baking powder and salt. In a medium bowl, beat egg yolks and add milk and canola oil. Stir in cherries and vanilla. Add cherry mixture to flour mixture and stir just to combine. In a medium bowl, beat egg whites until stiff. Fold egg whites into waffle batter. Spoon about 1 cup of batter mixture into the center of hot waffle iron and cook for about 4 minutes or until the light indicator on waffle iron goes off, or until waffle iron stops emitting steam. Serve immediately with butter and syrup.

6 waffles

MATÉ CHAI LATTE MUFFINS

I first sampled Maté Chai Latte from Pixie Maté at Expo East, and I knew immediately that I wanted to create a recipe using this beverage. I combined leftover cooked sweet potatoes with the complementary spices found in Maté Chai Latte (cinnamon, cloves and vanilla). The creation turned into muffins that Nick and I couldn't stop eating.

> *2 eggs*
> *½ cup cooked, mashed sweet potato*
> *½ cup Maté Chai Latte Concentrate (undiluted)*
> *¼ cup canola oil*
> *1¼ cups unbleached all-purpose flour*
> *½ cup brown sugar*
> *2 teaspoons baking powder*
> *1 teaspoon baking soda*
> *½ cup dried cranberries*
> *½ cup chopped walnuts*
> *butter*

Preheat oven to 350°F. Lightly oil a 12-cup muffin tin with cooking spray. In a large bowl, whisk eggs with sweet potato. Add Maté Chai Latte and canola oil and whisk until well combined. In a medium bowl, combine flour, brown sugar, baking powder and baking soda. Add dry ingredients to sweet potato mixture, and stir until combined. Fold in cranberries and walnuts. Fill muffin cups ¾ full with muffin mixture and bake for 15–17 minutes or until a toothpick inserted into center of a muffin comes out clean. Allow muffins to cool for about 5 minutes before removing from the tin. Serve with butter.

12 muffins

PLUM PERFECT PANCAKES

What better defines summer than a just-picked, sweet, juicy plum?

> ⅔ cup unbleached all-purpose flour
> ⅓ cup cornmeal
> ⅓ cup whole flax seeds, ground
> 1½ teaspoons baking powder
> 1½ teaspoons baking soda
> ½ teaspoon salt
> 1 cup milk
> 1 egg, separated
> 1 cup pitted and chopped fresh plums
> butter and syrup

In a large bowl, combine flour, cornmeal, ground flax seeds, baking powder, baking soda and salt. In a medium bowl, whisk the milk with the egg yolk. In another medium bowl, beat the egg white until firm peaks form. Add the milk/egg yolk mixture to the dry ingredients, and stir until combined. Fold in beaten egg white using a few rapid strokes. Gently fold in chopped plums. Coat a large skillet with canola oil and heat over a medium-high heat. To ensure oil is hot and ready to cook pancakes, sprinkle pan with water; if it sizzles, the oil is ready. Spoon about ¼ cup of the batter into the skillet for each pancake; a large skillet cooks about 3 at a time. Cook for about 2 minutes on each side or until light brown. Serve immediately with butter and syrup.

4 servings

Oven-Roasted Tomato Quiche

I developed this recipe when I was faced with an overabundance of ripe tomatoes. This quiche makes a beautiful presentation and it's delicious. While it is not our custom to overeat, my husband and I found ourselves coming back for thirds. Serve with a complementary tossed salad for a memorable meal. Oven-Roasted Tomatoes (see page 50) take about 45 minutes to roast. While I prefer a homemade crust, a good quality frozen shell will also work.

1⅛ cup unbleached all-purpose flour
½ teaspoon salt
¼ cup olive oil
2½–3 tablespoons cold water
1 tablespoon Dijon-style mustard
8 eggs
½ cup half-and-half
½ teaspoon salt
a sprinkling of cayenne pepper
3 cups grated cheddar cheese

In a medium bowl, combine flour and salt. Drizzle olive oil over flour and toss until flour mixture is coarse. Slowly drizzle in cold water. Knead dough a few times to fully incorporate ingredients. Add more water if dough doesn't come together or seems dry. Let dough rest for about 5 minutes. Lightly flour work surface and roll dough (if dough begins to resist, let it rest for about 5 minutes) until it is about 12 inches in diameter. Transfer to a 9-inch pie plate and flute edges. Spread mustard evenly over the bottom and sides of the unbaked crust. Preheat oven to 350°F. In a large bowl, beat eggs with a wire whisk. Add half-and-half, salt and cayenne pepper. Sprinkle 1 cup of cheese over mustard. Top the cheese with Oven-Roasted Tomatoes and top tomatoes with 1 cup of cheese. Pour egg mixture over cheese and top with remaining 1 cup of cheese. Bake quiche for 45 minutes or until lightly brown and knife inserted in center comes out clean. Allow quiche to cool for about 10 minutes before cutting.

6 to 8 servings

NUTRIENT-RICH BREAKFAST MUFFINS

To further enhance the multitude of flavors in these protein-packed, nutrient-rich muffins, spread hot-from-the-oven muffins with Better Butter (see page 45) or peanut butter. This muffin batter is thick, so thick that you might think these muffins would be heavy, but they'll be wonderfully dense and moist.

1 cup whole wheat flour
1 cup almonds, ground
⅓ cup cornmeal
⅓ cup soy flour
⅓ cup brown sugar
¼ cup wheat germ
1 teaspoon salt
1 teaspoon baking soda
½ cup rough chopped dried cranberries
½ cup chopped dried apricots
2 eggs
1 cup plain yogurt
½ cup canola oil
2 tablespoons grated orange peel
1 teaspoon vanilla

Preheat oven to 350°F. Generously oil a 12-capacity muffin tin with cooking spray. In a large bowl, combine wheat flour, ground almonds, cornmeal, soy flour, brown sugar, wheat germ, salt and baking soda. Stir in cranberries and apricots. In a medium bowl, combine eggs, yogurt, canola oil, orange peel and vanilla, then add to flour mixture. Combine ingredients until well blended. (The batter will be very thick.) Distribute evenly into muffin tin, and bake for 12–15 minutes or until toothpick inserted in the center of a muffin comes out clean. Cool muffins for about 5–10 minutes before removing from the pan.

12 muffins

CRUNCHY BANANA WAFFLES

Salba is an all-natural grain super food that now has a lot of health-conscious people taking notice. Salba is naturally rich in omega-3s, fiber, calcium and antioxidants, is gluten-free and has no trans-fats, few carbohydrates and is certified Non-GMO. It comes whole or ground; I prefer whole in this recipe because it produces an extra crunch. To round out the meal, serve with pork sausage, vegetarian sausage or bacon.

1¼ cups unbleached all-purpose flour
½ cup whole seed Salba
2 teaspoons baking powder
½ teaspoon salt
3 eggs, separated
½ cup canola oil
1½ cups milk
1 cup mashed ripe bananas (1–2 bananas)
butter and syrup

Prepare waffle iron according to directions. In a large bowl, combine flour, Salba, baking powder and salt. In a medium bowl, whisk egg yolks with oil and milk. Make a well in the center of the dry ingredients, pour in egg yolk mixture; and combine with a few swift strokes. Fold in banana. In a medium bowl, beat the egg whites until stiff. Fold into batter, just barely blending. When waffle iron is ready, spoon a heaping ½ cup of batter into the center, and cook until light brown or until waffle iron indicator light goes out. Serve immediately with butter and syrup.

5 waffles

Peach Pancakes

It was a warm July morning, and Nick and I had just left the farmers market with, among other fresh wonderful things, a bag of ripe, aromatic peaches. It was all I could do to contain myself from eating them all at once. Fortunately, visions of peach juice dripping down the front of my shirt kept me from indulging. Instead, I luxuriated in their sweet smell for the duration of the ride home, while listening to Nick talk about what awesome-tasting pancakes those peaches would make.

> *⅔ cup unbleached all-purpose flour*
> *⅓ cup cornmeal*
> *⅓ cup wheat germ*
> *1½ teaspoons baking powder*
> *1½ teaspoons baking soda*
> *½ teaspoon salt*
> *1 cup buttermilk*
> *1 egg, separated*
> *1 cup peeled, pitted and chopped peaches*
> *butter and syrup*

In a large bowl, combine flour, cornmeal, wheat germ, baking powder, baking soda and salt. In a medium bowl, whisk the buttermilk with the egg yolk. In another medium bowl, beat the egg white until firm peaks form. Add the buttermilk/egg yolk mixture to the dry ingredients, and stir with swift strokes. Fold in beaten egg white and peaches. Coat a large skillet with canola oil and heat over a medium-high heat. To ensure the oil is hot enough to cook the pancakes, sprinkle pan with water, and when oil sizzles, spoon batter into skillet (about ¼ cup per pancake). A large skillet cooks about 3 pancakes at a time. Cook for approximately 2 minutes on each side or until light brown. Serve immediately with butter and syrup.

4 servings

Naturally-Sweetened Blueberry Muffins

When blueberries are in season, I just can't seem to get my fill of them. These sweet, healthy berries boast impressive amounts of fiber and nutrients. I prefer to grind whole flax seeds and whole seed Salba just prior to use. A coffee grinder works perfectly for this.

> 1½ cups unbleached all-purpose flour
> ¼ cup whole flax seeds, ground
> ¼ cup whole seed Salba, ground
> 2 teaspoons baking powder
> ½ teaspoon salt
> 1 egg
> ½ cup milk
> ½ cup canola oil
> 1 teaspoon vanilla
> 2 cups fresh blueberries

Preheat oven to 400°F. Lightly oil 10 cups in a 12-cup capacity muffin tin with cooking spray. In a large bowl, combine flour, ground flax seeds, ground Salba, baking powder and salt. In a medium bowl, whisk the egg with milk, canola oil and vanilla. Make a well in the center of the dry ingredients and pour in the milk mixture. Combine with a few swift strokes. In a small bowl, mash a ½ cup of the blueberries. Add the mashed berries and the remaining blueberries to the batter. Stir gently until combined. Divide batter among the 10 prepared muffin cups. Bake for about 12–15 minutes or until a toothpick inserted in the center of a muffin comes out clean. Serve immediately.

10 muffins

FRENCH-TOASTED CROISSANTS WITH BLUEBERRY SAUCE

This is just the type of recipe I like to prepare when hosting a breakfast or brunch. No rushing around trying to feed hungry guests; the croissant portion of this dish must be assembled the day before you plan to serve it. To round out the meal, serve with pork sausage, vegetarian sausage or bacon.

6 ready-made mini croissants, sliced lengthwise
4 eggs
½ cup milk
1 teaspoon vanilla
1 teaspoon cinnamon
1½ cups fresh or frozen blueberries
½ cup sugar
butter (optional)

Arrange croissant halves in a single layer in an 11 by 7-inch (2-quart) baking dish. It will be a bit crowded, but the croissants will sort themselves out while marinating overnight. In a medium bowl, whisk eggs with milk; and add vanilla and whisk until well blended. Pour ½ of the egg/milk mixture over croissant halves; turn croissants over to coat completely. Turn halves over and top with croissant top and pour remaining egg/milk mixture over croissants. Sprinkle cinnamon evenly over croissants. Cover and refrigerate overnight.

Remove croissants from refrigerator 30 minutes prior to baking. Preheat oven to 350°F. In a medium saucepan over moderately low heat, combine blueberries with sugar. When sugar has dissolved and blueberries have broken down (about 15 minutes), remove from heat and spoon blueberry topping over croissants. Bake for 30 minutes. Serve immediately. Top with butter if desired.

4 to 6 servings

MANGO AND CARDAMOM COFFEE CAKE WITH ALMOND STREUSEL

I am partial to mangoes; I love how their sweet, slick fleshiness melts in your mouth. Mangoes taste like a cross between a peach and an apricot, with pineapple undertones.

1½ cups unbleached all-purpose flour
½ cup sugar
2 teaspoons baking powder
½ teaspoon baking soda
½ teaspoon cardamom
¼ teaspoon salt
1 cup sour cream
2 eggs
1 cup peeled and chopped mango (about 1 large)
2 tablespoons unbleached all-purpose flour
⅓ cup sugar
2 tablespoons butter, cut into chunks
¼ cup sliced or slivered almonds

Preheat oven to 350°F. In a large bowl, combine flour, sugar, baking powder, baking soda, cardamom and salt. In a medium bowl, whisk sour cream with eggs, and whisk until well blended. Add mango. Add mango mixture to flour mixture and stir until fully incorporated. Transfer batter into a lightly oiled 8 x 8 x 2-inch pan.

In a small bowl, combine flour and sugar, and add chunks of butter and blend using your fingers until streusel crumbles. Sprinkle streusel crumbles evenly over cake, and top with sliced almonds. Bake for 35–40 minutes or until light brown. Serve immediately.

8 servings

BUCKWHEAT PARSNIP WAFFLES

Despite its name, buckwheat is wheat-free. It's actually a fruit seed that is rich in nutrients and gluten-free, making buckwheat flour a healthy choice. While parsnips are a key ingredient in these waffles, no one will ever know.

1¼ cups unbleached all-purpose flour
½ cup buckwheat flour
2 teaspoons baking powder
½ teaspoon salt
3 eggs, separated
½ cup canola oil
1½ cups milk
1 cup peeled and shredded parsnips
butter and syrup

Prepare waffle iron according to directions. In a large bowl, combine flour, buckwheat flour, baking powder and salt. In a medium bowl, whisk egg yolks with oil and milk. Make a well in the center of the dry ingredients and pour in egg yolk/milk mixture. Combine with a few swift strokes. Fold in parsnips. In a medium bowl, beat egg whites until stiff; fold into batter, just barely blending. When waffle iron is ready, spoon a heaping ½ cup of the batter into the center of the waffle iron. Cook until light brown or until waffle iron indicator light goes out. Serve immediately with butter and syrup.

5 waffles

Vegan Sausage and Spinach Quiche

Gimme Lean Meat Free Ground Sausage is the most authentic tasting vegan sausage I've discovered. You can successfully serve this one-dish meal without an accompaniment, but I prefer to complement it with tomatoes—stewed in the winter, sliced fresh in the summer. If you're pressed for time, a store-bought crust can be used.

1⅛ cups unbleached all-purpose flour
½ teaspoon salt
¼ cup olive oil
2½–3 tablespoons cold water

In a medium bowl, combine flour and salt. Drizzle olive oil over flour and toss until flour mixture is coarse. Slowly drizzle in cold water. Add more water if dough doesn't come together or seems dry. Knead dough a few times to fully incorporate ingredients. Let dough rest for about 5 minutes. Lightly flour work surface and roll dough (if dough begins to resist, let it rest for about 5 minutes), until it's about 12 inches in diameter. Transfer to a 9-inch pie plate and flute edges.

1 tablespoon olive oil
1 cup finely chopped onion
½ package (about 7 ounces) meat free ground sausage
8 eggs
½ cup half-and-half
½ teaspoon salt
½ teaspoon oregano
½ teaspoon marjoram
½ teaspoon thyme
½ teaspoon dry mustard
a dash of cayenne pepper
3 cups shredded cheddar cheese
16 ounces frozen chopped spinach, defrosted, drained, and squeezed dry

Preheat oven to 350°F. Heat olive oil in a medium sauté pan over moderate heat, and add onion and ground sausage, and cook until sausage has browned; remove from heat. In a large bowl, whisk eggs with half-and-half, salt, oregano, marjoram, thyme, dry mustard and cayenne pepper. Sprinkle 1 cup of shredded cheese in the bottom of the unbaked quiche crust. Top the cheese with ½ of the drained spinach and ½ of the ground sausage mixture. Sprinkle with 1 cup of cheese. Top with remaining ½ of the spinach and remaining ground sausage mixture. Pour egg mixture evenly over the spinach/sausage mixture, and top with remaining cup of cheese. Bake for 45 minutes. Allow quiche to sit for 10 minutes before serving.

6 servings

Chestnut Pancakes

I first spotted chestnut flour several years ago while on a tour of Vann Spices, a Baltimore-based spice company. Intrigued, I left with a bag, determined to create recipes using this new (to me) flour. The bag sat in my pantry until one blustery winter morning when Nick announced his desire for pancakes. Running low on all-purpose flour, I set out on a mission: to develop a chestnut flour pancake.

> *1 cup unbleached all-purpose flour*
> *½ cup chestnut flour*
> *½ cup Winter Sippers Hot Buttered Rum Mix*
> *2 teaspoons baking powder*
> *1 teaspoon salt*
> *1 cup buttermilk*
> *1 egg*
> *¼ cup canola oil*
> *butter and syrup*

In a large bowl, combine flour, chestnut flour, Winter Sippers Hot Buttered Rum Mix, baking powder and salt. In a medium bowl, add buttermilk, egg and canola oil, and whisk until well blended. Add the buttermilk mixture to the flour mixture, and stir (using swift strokes) until fully incorporated. Heat canola oil in a large skillet over moderate heat. Drop batter (about ¼ cup per pancake) onto skillet. Batter will be very thick. Cook for about 2 minutes on each side or until lightly brown. Serve immediately with butter and syrup.

4 servings

Introducing

SOUPS

This is the largest section in *Tasting the Seasons,* and with good reason. I learned to love soup at a very young age. My mother prepared three meals a day, seven days a week, for our family of seven, working within the confines of a limited budget. So one-pot meals allowed her to not only stretch her budget dollars, but also let her imagination run free. She was known to put whatever leftovers she found in the refrigerator into a pot and turn it into the most amazing meal.

I enthusiastically adopted my mother's method for building one-pot meals and have created some unique and some familiar combinations that I've preserved as recipes—recipes that have become huge favorites among family and friends. Homemade soup and homemade bread are two of my favorite foods to serve when entertaining, and Nick and I are known for the soup-sampling parties we host. I typically prepare three different kinds of soup and a few batches of Focaccia (see page 220). Guests always leave feeling completely satisfied and so appreciative of the time spent cooking for them. Besides, soup-sampling parties are not your run-of-the-mill type of party, and new party themes are always much anticipated, as well as lots of fun.

If you're not so inclined (or don't have the time) to make your own stock, many of the recipes in this section call for a vegetable bouillon cube. Rapunzel brand makes a delicious, organic, full-flavored vegetable bouillon cube with sea salt that I recommend. Other recipes call for chicken broth, and I tested many brands before I chose Imagine as my preferred brand; I found it to taste the closest to homemade. For my vegetarian readers, I'd like to note here that you can generally substitute vegetable bouillon cubes in any recipe calling for chicken broth.

Soup is a combination of meat, seafood, poultry and/or vegetables and fruits combined with milk, water or broth as the liquid base. Soups can be served hot or cold, thick or thin, savory or sweet, as a first course, the main meal, or in the case of Whirled Peaches with Amaretto (see page 247), as a delicious, refreshing dessert.

Stew also uses meat, seafood, poultry and/or vegetables as a base, but these ingredients are simmered for several hours, tenderizing all ingredients and turning out a thick, rich and hearty mixture.

Chowder is a thick soup often made with potatoes, bacon and onions with either a dairy-based or tomato-based broth, as in traditional Manhattan clam chowder or ChickBanzo Chowder (see page 114). Seafood and vegetables usually round out this dish.

77

Bisque is a rich, smooth and creamy soup made using shellfish, chicken and/or vegetables and often thickened with flour.

Most soups age beautifully; you should definitely consider making them a day or two before you plan to serve them. Creamier, puréed soups and those soups that include flour and/or beans tend to thicken with time. It may be necessary to add liquid to get the original or desired consistency.

I tend to serve puréed soups or lighter soups as a first course. I've found that ½-cup servings are more than enough if the soup is followed by a main meal, sides and dessert. When you're serving heartier soups, consideration should always be given as to how hearty the appetites are of your guests and whether or not this heartier dish will be the first course or the main meal.

Recipe Overview

HEARTY SOUPS

Poached Mozzarella and Tomato Soup over Grilled Curry Bread

Indian Meatball Stew with Curried Cucumber Yogurt

Vegetable Barley Soup with Herbes de Provence

Chickpea and Mushroom Soup with Vegetables

Sweet Potato and Hominy Soup with Shrimp

Curried Carrot Soup with Coconut Shrimp

Apple Cinnamon Butternut Squash Soup

Gingered Parsnip and Coconut Soup

Eggplant and Black Lentil Stew

Chunky Peanut Butter Soup

Italian Sausage Bread Soup

My Mother's Favorite Soup

Mushroom and Barley Soup

Christmas Lima Bean Soup

Cheese Tortellini Chowder

Purée of Cauliflower Soup

Cream of Kohlrabi Soup

Curried Broccoli Soup

Catfish Chowder

French Onion Soup

Braised Pot Roast Stew

POACHED MOZZARELLA AND TOMATO SOUP OVER GRILLED CURRY BREAD

Remember those fabulous lunches at your grandmother's house when you dipped your grilled cheese sandwich into a bowl of tomato soup? Flash forward a couple of decades. This is a harmonious combination of flavors that always receives rave reviews. Ciabatta bread is an airy, holey bread that grills beautifully.

> 2 tablespoons olive oil
> 1 cup finely minced onion
> 2 garlic cloves, finely minced
> 2 cans (28 ounces each) diced tomatoes
> 4 teaspoons sugar
> 1 teaspoon oregano
> 1 teaspoon basil
> 1 teaspoon salt
> ¼–½ teaspoon red pepper flakes, according to your preference
> freshly ground black pepper, to taste
> 2 teaspoons curry powder
> 4–6 tablespoons butter, softened
> 8 slices (½ inch) ciabatta bread
> 8 slices (¼ inch) mozzarella cheese

Heat olive oil in a large soup pot over moderate heat and add onion and garlic and sauté until onion is transparent. Add tomatoes, sugar, oregano, basil, salt, red pepper flakes and black pepper. Reduce heat to simmer and cook uncovered for about a ½ hour.

In a small bowl, combine curry powder and butter and mix until well blended. On a sheet of parchment paper, lay out 8 slices of bread. Spread butter mixture evenly over both sides of each slice. Cover the bottom of a large skillet or sauté pan with canola oil. Heat pan over moderately high heat. Add slices of bread (in batches of 3–4) and grill on each side until golden. While the bread is grilling, place 3–4 slices of the mozzarella (the same number as the number of pieces of bread) on top of the tomato soup in the large pot; cheese should not be overlapping. Cover soup for a few minutes so cheese can soften; cheese should keep its shape.

Transfer grilled bread slices to shallow bowls. Carefully lift each slice of mozzarella from tomato soup with a flat-bottomed slotted spoon and place on top of bread slice. Repeat bread grilling/cheese poaching process until all bread and mozzarella slices are cooked. Ladle tomato soup over each mozzarella-topped slice of bread and drizzle olive oil over contents of each bowl. Serve immediately.

8 servings

INDIAN MEATBALL STEW WITH CURRIED CUCUMBER YOGURT

This recipe is an excellent choice if you enjoy spicy, Indian cuisine. If you have an Indian grocer in your neighborhood, you won't have any problem finding naan, the popular Indian flat bread that is traditionally served with this cuisine. You can also find naan in the bakery department of many grocery stores nationwide.

2 eggs
½ teaspoon salt
⅓ cup bread crumbs
½ cup chopped, pitted prunes
1 pound lean ground beef
2 tablespoons olive oil
1 medium onion, minced
2 garlic cloves, minced
2 tablespoons Tandoori spice blend
2 cups water
1 can (28 ounces) diced tomatoes
½ cup fresh minced parsley
naan

In a large bowl, whisk eggs with salt and add bread crumbs and prunes. Add ground beef to egg/crumb mixture and combine well. Form mixture into bite-size meatballs (about 18–20) and transfer to a platter large enough to accommodate the meatballs.

Heat olive oil in a large pot over moderate heat and add onion and sauté until translucent. Add garlic and sauté for an additional 1 minute. Add Tandoori spices and sauté for 1 minute. Add water, tomatoes and parsley and bring mixture to a gentle boil. Reduce heat, add meatballs and cover and simmer for 30 minutes. Meanwhile, keep the stew warm while you prepare the Curried Cucumber Yogurt. Once you've prepared Curried Cucumber Yogurt, heat the naan according to package directions.

CURRIED CUCUMBER YOGURT
½ teaspoon red curry paste (or ¼ teaspoon if you're sensitive to spicy)
¾ cup plain yogurt
¼ cup sour cream
1 cup peeled, seeded, shredded cucumber
¼ cup minced green onion
⅛ cup grated coconut
½ teaspoon salt

In a medium bowl, combine red curry paste with yogurt and sour cream. Add cucumber, green onion, coconut and salt; combine until well blended.

Ladle hot stew into bowls and pass the Curried Cucumber Yogurt to your guests along with the warm naan.

6 servings

VEGETABLE BARLEY SOUP WITH HERBES DE PROVENCE

Herbes de Provence is a classic mix of herbs most commonly used in the southern region of Provence, France: a mix that includes winter savory, thyme, rosemary, basil, tarragon, and lavender flowers. It's the lavender that gives this herb combination its distinct flavor, a flavor that suits the ingredients in this soup beautifully. For this recipe, I used quick cooking barley, which saves time, but doesn't sacrifice the wonderful, chewy texture that barley is known for. As with many hearty soups, this one improves with age.

1 tablespoon olive oil
½ cup chopped onion
2 garlic cloves, minced
½ pound fresh mushrooms, sliced
4 cups water
1 cup julienned carrots
1 cup sliced celery
2 vegetable bouillon cubes
1 tablespoon cooking sherry
1 teaspoon Herbes de Provence
½ teaspoon salt
1½ cups quick cooking barley, cooked according to package directions

Heat olive oil in a large pot over moderate heat. Add onion and cook for about 2–3 minutes or until translucent. Add garlic and mushrooms and cook until mushrooms are tender. Add water, carrots, celery and vegetable cubes. Bring to a boil, cover, reduce heat to simmer and cook until carrots and celery are tender, about 5 minutes. Add sherry, Herbes de Provence, salt and barley. Serve immediately.

6 servings

CHICKPEA AND MUSHROOM SOUP WITH VEGETABLES

Not only is this soup simple to assemble, it's nutritious, requires very little cooking time, and it's beautiful. For a delicious meal, serve with a hearty loaf of bread or Oatmeal Rolls (see page 224).

2 tablespoons olive oil
3 garlic cloves, sliced
1½ cups sliced fresh mushrooms
2 cups chicken broth
1 can (14 ounces) chickpeas (garbanzo beans)
1 can (28 ounces) diced tomatoes
10 ounces frozen spinach, thawed
salt and pepper, to taste
feta cheese, crumbled
Kalamata black olives, pitted

In a large soup pot, heat oil over medium heat and sauté garlic and mushrooms. Cook, stirring frequently, until mushrooms are tender, about 3–5 minutes. Add chicken broth, chickpeas, tomatoes and spinach. Cover, raise the temperature a notch, bring soup to a boil, and then reduce heat to simmer. Season the soup with salt and pepper. Ladle soup into bowls. Serve immediately and pass the feta cheese and black olives to your guests.

6 servings

SWEET POTATO AND HOMINY SOUP WITH SHRIMP

When I was a child, my father's parents ate hominy all the time, and I loved it. Even though it doesn't rank too high on the nutritional charts, I couldn't resist adding these pure-white miniature balls to this colorful and tasty pot of soup. Cut and cube the avocado just before serving.

> *2 cups peeled and cubed sweet potato*
> *1½ cups water*
> *1 vegetable bouillon cube*
> *1 cup sliced celery*
> *1 cup chopped white onion*
> *1 can (14 ounces) chopped tomatoes*
> *1 can (8½ ounces) hominy*
> *1 can (15 ounces) black beans*
> *2 cups steamed, peeled, deveined and cut up shrimp*
> *3 tablespoons cooking sherry*
> *2 avocados, cut into bite-size cubes*

In a medium pot, boil sweet potato cubes in just enough water to cover. In a large pot, bring 1½ cups of water to a boil, add the vegetable cube and stir until the cube has dissolved. Add celery, onion and tomatoes and cook until vegetables are tender, about 5 minutes. Add cooked sweet potato, hominy, black beans and shrimp. Add sherry and simmer for 10 minutes. Ladle into soup bowls and top with avocado cubes. Serve immediately.

6 servings

CURRIED CARROT SOUP
WITH COCONUT SHRIMP

This is one of those recipes you'll come back to again and again. It's a great choice if you're having an important dinner party and want to present a unique combination that is rich with flavor. It needs nothing more than a tossed green salad and slices of good-quality bread or corn muffins. It's best to cook the shrimp just prior to serving.

2 tablespoons canola oil
2 cups sliced white onion
4 teaspoons curry powder
6 cups chicken broth
8 medium sliced carrots (about 5–6 cups)
1 can (14 ounces) coconut milk
1 cup natural chunky peanut butter
1–2 teaspoon salt
24 count large raw shrimp, peeled, deveined and cut into chunks
2 tablespoons olive oil
½–1 teaspoon kosher salt
1 cup shredded coconut

In a large pot, heat olive oil over moderate heat, add onion and sauté until translucent. Add curry powder and sauté until fragrant, about 1 minute. Add chicken broth and carrots, bring mixture to a boil, cover, reduce heat and cook until carrots are tender, about 15 minutes. Transfer mixture to a food processor and purée in batches until smooth; transfer puréed batches to a large bowl. Add coconut milk, peanut butter and salt to the last batch to be puréed and process until velvety smooth. Add to puréed carrot/onion mixture and combine until fully blended. Transfer blended mixture back into the large soup pot, cover and simmer until shrimp are ready to serve. Preheat oven to 425°F. In medium bowl, toss shrimp with olive oil and salt. Let stand for 10 minutes. Toss shrimp with coconut and place in a single layer on a parchment-lined baking sheet. Bake for about 10 minutes or until shrimp are firm and coconut is slightly brown/black. Divide the soup into 8 shallow serving bowls and top each with 6 chunks of shrimp. Serve immediately.

8 servings

APPLE CINNAMON BUTTERNUT SQUASH SOUP

This soup is a fall classic!

1 medium butternut squash
2 tablespoons butter
1 cup chopped onion
1 teaspoon cinnamon
1½ cups sliced carrots
1 cup sliced celery
1½ cups unpeeled, sliced apple
1½ cups chicken broth
1 cup milk
1 teaspoon salt

Preheat oven to 350°F. Slice squash in half length-wise and spoon out seeds. Place squash cut side down in a baking dish large enough to accommodate the squash. Add about 1 inch of water (enough so that squash is slightly submerged) and bake for about 45 minutes or until fork-tender. When cool enough to handle, scrape squash from skin. In a large pot over moderate heat, melt butter and sauté onion until transparent. Add cinnamon and sauté for about 1 minute or until fragrant. Add carrots, celery, apple and chicken broth and bring to a boil; cover, reduce heat and cook for about 30 minutes or until vegetables and apple slices are tender. Allow soup to cool slightly. Transfer to a food processor or blender and purée in batches; transfer puréed batches into a large bowl. Add squash, milk and salt to the final batch to be puréed and process until smooth. Transfer puréed squash mixture into the large bowl and whisk until well blended. Transfer blended mixture back into original large pot; simmer until ready to serve. Serve immediately.

6 servings

GINGERED PARSNIP AND COCONUT SOUP

Parsnips are one of my favorite vegetables. I like their mild, mellow and naturally sweet flavor. Whenever I serve this soup "Mmmmm's" and "Oh, wow's" always fill the room.

>   2 tablespoons butter
>   1 cup chopped white onion
>   3 cups water
>   2 vegetable bouillon cubes
>   2 pounds parsnips, peeled and cut into chunks
>   1 teaspoon ginger
>   1 teaspoon salt
>   2 cups milk
>   1 can (14 ounces) coconut milk

In a large pot over medium heat, melt butter and sauté onion until translucent. Add water, vegetable cubes and parsnips. Cover, bring to a boil, lower heat and cook parsnips until tender, about 30–40 minutes. Purée mixture in a food processor or blender in batches and transfer mixture into a large bowl as it's puréed. Add ginger, salt and milk to the last batch to be puréed and transfer back into original large pot. Transfer puréed mixture into the pot; add coconut milk and stir until well blended. Simmer until heated through. Serve immediately.

8 servings

EGGPLANT AND BLACK LENTIL STEW

I have the same affection for eggplant that eggplant has for oil, and the latter is the secret to this delicious stew. Serve with either a tossed salad and Free-Form Country Bread (see page 225) or grilled cheese sandwiches. This stew thickens with age, whether you refrigerate it overnight or simply simmer it for a longer period of time.

1 eggplant cut into 1-inch slices (1½ pounds)
2 teaspoons coarse salt
½ cup black lentils
2 cups water
1½ cups thinly sliced white onion
1¼ cups tomato sauce
½ cup minced fresh parsley
¼ teaspoon crushed red pepper
½ cup extra virgin olive oil

Place eggplant slices in a single layer on a rimmed baking sheet. Pierce each slice several times with a fork; sprinkle with salt. Let stand 1 hour. Place lentils in a large soup pot and cover them with 2 cups of water. Bring to a boil, reduce heat, cover and simmer until lentils are tender, about 20–25 minutes. Cube eggplant and add to lentils. Add onions, tomato sauce, parsley, red pepper and olive oil and stir to combine. (The stew will produce its own liquid during cooking.) Bring mixture to a gentle boil, cover, reduce heat and simmer 1 hour or until eggplant is fork tender. Serve immediately.

6 servings

CHUNKY PEANUT BUTTER SOUP

When my mother passed this recipe on to me, she said it was an adaptation of the many recipes she had collected from southern restaurants where this surprising combination is often served. Peanut soup is a classic that the American colonists used to enjoy and remains a staple today in Williamsburg restaurants and taverns.

½ stick (¼ cup) butter
½ cup minced celery
½ cup minced white onion
½ cup unbleached all-purpose flour
5 cups chicken broth
2 cups natural chunky peanut butter
1 cup heavy cream

Melt butter in a medium sauté pan over moderate heat and sauté celery and onion until tender. Slowly whisk in flour (it will grab the celery and onion very quickly). Add the chicken broth 1 cup at a time and whisk until well blended. Reduce heat to simmer and whisk in peanut butter. Add cream and whisk until ingredients are fully blended. Serve hot or cold.

6 servings

ITALIAN SAUSAGE BREAD SOUP

This is a hearty soup that needs nothing more than a nice bottle of Chianti and good company.

> *3 cups chicken broth*
> *3 cups water*
> *5 cups sliced celery*
> *salt and pepper, to taste*
> *1½ pounds Italian sausage links*
> *6 slices (about 1-inch thick) traditional Italian bread*
> *6 hard-boiled eggs*
> *shaved Pecorino cheese*

In a medium pot, bring chicken broth and water to a boil. Reduce heat, add celery, and cook until celery is tender, about 10 minutes. Season the mixture with salt and pepper. Lightly coat the bottom of a large skillet with canola oil. Cook sausage links over moderately low heat until brown and cooked through. When cool enough to handle, thinly slice on the diagonal about ¼–½-inch thick. Place one slice of bread in the bottom of 6 shallow soup bowls. Increase heat under broth and bring to a gentle boil. Meanwhile, rough-chop each egg individually and place chopped pieces over bread in each bowl. Divide sausage evenly and add to the bread and egg. Top each bowl with a few shavings of cheese. Carefully ladle boiling hot broth into each bowl. Serve immediately.

6 servings

My Mother's Favorite Soup

This soup is a clever combination created by my mother. The addition of hard-boiled eggs in this delicious, nutritious, complete-meal-in-a-bowl recipe is what makes this soup unique. The egg whites are chopped and added to the soup and the yolks are combined with some of the hot broth and then added to the soup. The result is a creamy mixture that thickens the soup to perfection.

5 cups water
3 cups peeled and cubed potatoes
1 cup chopped celery
1 cup sliced carrot
1 cup chopped white onion
½ cup minced fresh parsley
2 vegetable bouillon cubes
4 tablespoons butter
1 teaspoon salt
freshly ground black pepper, to taste
4 hard-boiled eggs

In a large pot, bring water to a boil and add potatoes and cook until just slightly tender. Add celery, carrot and onion to the potatoes. Reduce heat and cook until potatoes and vegetables are fork-tender. Add parsley, vegetable cubes, butter, salt and pepper. Cut hard-boiled eggs in half, remove yolks and place them in a medium bowl. Chop egg whites and add to soup. Ladle about ¼–½ cup hot broth over egg yolks and stir until creamy. Add yolk mixture to soup and stir until well blended. Serve immediately.

6 servings

MUSHROOM AND BARLEY SOUP

I was invited to a friend's house for dinner, and her mom served us steaming bowls filled with barley and mushrooms. This soup is a rendition of hers and is perfect on a cold, wintry night. Better Feather Biscuits slathered with Better Butter (see Index for recipes) are perfect complements.

1 tablespoon olive oil
½ cup chopped onion
6–8 fresh white mushrooms, sliced
4 cups chicken broth
1 cup water
1 medium carrot, sliced
1 stalk celery, sliced
1½ cups chopped cooked white meat chicken
½ cup raw barley, cooked according to directions (about 1½ cup yield)
½ cup minced fresh parsley
½ teaspoon salt
freshly ground black pepper, to taste

Heat olive oil in a large pot over moderate heat and sauté onion and mushrooms until tender. Add chicken broth, water, sliced carrot and celery and bring mixture to a boil. Cover, reduce heat to simmer and cook until carrots and celery are tender, about 5–10 minutes. Add chicken, barley, parsley and salt and pepper. Simmer until heated through, about 10 minutes. Serve immediately.

8 servings

CHRISTMAS LIMA BEAN SOUP

I was thrilled to discover Christmas lima beans for many reasons. They have a long history in American cuisine, dating back to the 1840s. They're beautiful: a cream-colored bean with splashes of maroon. And they're an excellent source of fiber and loaded with protein. If you can't find Christmas lima beans, just about any other hearty bean works. This soup thickens as it cooks, so you may need to add additional liquid to keep it at a desired consistency. Arugula Salad with Halloumi (see page 176) is a wonderful complement to this hearty soup.

12 ounces Christmas lima beans
4 cups water
6 cups water
3 vegetable bouillon cubes
1 tablespoon olive oil
1 cup chopped white onion
2 garlic cloves, minced
2 cups water
2 cups julienned carrots
1 cup chopped celery
1½ cups cooked rice
½ cup minced fresh parsley
1 teaspoon salt
freshly ground black pepper, to taste

Soak beans in 4 cups of water overnight. Discard soaking water. Transfer beans to a large pot and add 6 cups of water. Bring beans and water to a boil over high heat. Cover, reduce heat to simmer and cook beans until tender, about 1 hour. Add vegetable cubes to the cooked beans and allow the cubes to dissolve in the hot bean water. Heat olive oil in large pot over medium-high heat and add onion and cook until translucent. Add garlic and cook for an additional 2–3 minutes. Add water to the onions and garlic and bring mixture to a boil. Add carrots and celery, cover and cook until vegetables are fork-tender, about 5–10 minutes. Add the vegetables to the beans and stir in the rice and the parsley. Season the soup with salt and pepper. Serve immediately.

8 servings

CHEESE TORTELLINI CHOWDER

My taste-testers ranked this as one of the best chowders they had ever eaten. This chowder gets thicker with time; you may need to add more chicken broth.

>   *2 tablespoons butter*
>   *½ cup chopped onion*
>   *½ cup sliced celery*
>   *½ cup chopped red pepper*
>   *½ cup shredded carrots*
>   *½ cup corn*
>   *2 tablespoons unbleached all-purpose flour*
>   *2 cups chicken broth*
>   *1 cup white wine*
>   *1 cup water*
>   *1 vegetable bouillon cube*
>   *⅛ cup cooking sherry*
>   *½ teaspoon salt*
>   *freshly ground black pepper, to taste*
>   *1 cup heavy cream*
>   *10 ounces tri-color cheese tortellini*
>   *2 tablespoons minced fresh parsley*

Melt butter in a large pot over moderate heat and sauté onions, celery, red pepper, carrots and corn. Cook until tender, about 10 minutes. Whisk in flour (it will grab the vegetables very quickly) and slowly add chicken broth, whisking constantly. Add white wine, water and vegetable cube and stir until cube dissolves. Add sherry, salt, pepper, cream, tortellini and parsley and stir to combine. Simmer until heated through. Serve immediately.

6 servings

PURÉE OF CAULIFLOWER SOUP

An impromptu visit from good friends, Art and Sue Grotz, prompted me to assemble a celebratory lunch. I paired this mellow-tasting, velvety-smooth soup with Traditional Spinach Salad. As the afternoon light faded into dusk, we sipped deep, garnet-colored Sangria studded with fresh seasonal fruit (see Index for recipes) while we caught up on Art and Sue's latest inland waterway adventure.

> 2½ cups water
> 1 large head cauliflower, cut into uniform pieces
> 4 tablespoons butter
> ½ cup chopped white onion
> 2 tablespoons unbleached all-purpose flour
> 1 cup chicken broth
> 1 cup milk
> 2 vegetable bouillon cubes
> 2 cups cauliflower water
> shredded cheddar cheese

In a large pot with a steamer, bring 2½ cups of water to a boil, add cauliflower and steam until fork-tender. Transfer cauliflower and cauliflower water to a large bowl. Remove steamer, and in the same large pot over moderate heat, melt butter and sauté onion until tender. Whisk in flour and slowly add chicken broth. Add milk and vegetable cubes and allow vegetable cubes to dissolve. Add cauliflower water and cauliflower. In a food processor or blender, purée soup in batches; transfer puréed batches into a large bowl. After final batch is puréed, transfer soup back into the original large pot. Simmer until hot. Serve immediately and pass the cheddar cheese to your guests.

6 servings

CREAM OF KOHLRABI SOUP

This humble (yet quite unusual-looking) vegetable is a member of the cabbage family, and its edible, bulbous stem has a mild, sweet taste when cooked. While vegetable bouillon cubes are used in this recipe, chicken broth can be substituted with equally great results. And yes, I swear, the plural of kohlrabi is kohlrabies.

> *3 tablespoons butter*
> *1 medium white onion, chopped*
> *3 cups water*
> *2 vegetable bouillon cubes*
> *4–6 small kohlrabies (about 3 cups), peeled and cubed*
> *1 pound potatoes, unpeeled and cubed*
> *1 cup half-and-half*
> *1½ teaspoons salt*
> *freshly ground black pepper, to taste*

In a large pot over moderate heat, melt the butter and sauté the onion until tender. Add water and vegetable cubes. Bring mixture to a boil and stir until cubes have dissolved. Add kohlrabies and potatoes (the water won't cover the vegetables), reduce heat to simmer and cook for about 20–30 minutes or until vegetables are tender. Allow soup to cool slightly. Purée soup in batches; as you purée, transfer batches to a large bowl. In the last batch to be puréed, add half-and-half and salt and pepper to taste. Transfer all puréed soup back into the original large pot and stir until well blended. Simmer until heated through. Serve immediately.

8 servings

CURRIED BROCCOLI SOUP

If you're not a fan of broccoli, or you can't get your family to eat this nutrient-rich vegetable, no one will ever know that the main ingredient in this zesty soup is broccoli. Even the color won't give it away, because the tomato paste turns this soup into a beautiful shade of pumpkin.

2 tablespoons butter
1 cup coarsely chopped white onion
1 cup coarsely chopped celery
2 teaspoons curry powder
1 can (6 ounces) tomato paste
3 cups water
1 vegetable bouillon cube
6–7 cups broccoli, uniform pieces (florets and peeled stems)
1 cup heavy cream
1 teaspoon salt
2 tablespoons cooking sherry

In a large pot over moderate heat, melt butter and sauté onion and celery until tender. Stir in curry powder and cook for about 1 minute. Add tomato paste, water and vegetable cube and stir until tomato paste is incorporated with water. Add broccoli and cover pot. Reduce heat to simmer and cook for about 30 minutes or until broccoli is fork-tender. Allow soup to cool slightly before puréeing in a food processor. Purée soup in batches and as you purée, transfer mixture to a large bowl. Add cream, salt and sherry to the last batch to be puréed and transfer to the original soup pot. Add the puréed mixture from the large bowl to soup pot and stir until well blended. Simmer soup until heated through. Serve immediately.

6 servings

CATFISH CHOWDER

This soup was created as a token of affection for my very first catering clients, Serena and Jerry Baum.

1 tablespoon butter
2 cups peeled and cubed potatoes
2 cups sliced celery
2 cups sliced white onion
1 teaspoon salt
1 teaspoon dried dill weed
2 tablespoons unbleached all-purpose flour
1½ cups boiling water
1 pound catfish, cut into 1-inch pieces
½ cup white wine
1 cup milk
¼ cup minced fresh parsley
freshly ground black pepper, to taste

In a large pot over medium heat, melt butter; add potatoes, celery, onion, salt and dill and sauté for about 5 minutes, stirring frequently. Add flour and cook for about 1 minute. Add the boiling water to the vegetables, cover and reduce heat to simmer and cook until vegetables are tender, about 10–15 minutes. Add the catfish and white wine. Cook until fish is opaque and starts to flake, about 15 minutes. Stir in milk and parsley and season with black pepper. Serve immediately.

6 servings

FRENCH ONION SOUP

Traditional French onion soup is often prepared with stock made from beef bones, a method that is sometimes too lengthy for today's busy schedules. Imagine brand Organic Beef Flavored Broth has an authentic beef broth flavor. The result here is a traditional, French onion soup that your guests will think you spent hours preparing.

2 tablespoons butter
8 cups thinly sliced yellow onions
4 tablespoons cooking sherry
4 cups beef broth
1 teaspoon salt
freshly ground black pepper, to taste
4 slices day-old French bread rounds
butter, softened
freshly grated Parmesan cheese
Gruyère or Swiss cheese, sliced to desired thickness

In a large pot over moderate heat, melt butter; add onions and sauté for 15–20 minutes or until onions begin to brown. Add cooking sherry, beef broth, salt and pepper. Cover soup, bring to a boil, reduce heat and simmer for about 30 minutes. Spread French bread rounds with butter and top each round with grated Parmesan cheese. Toast until light brown in either a 350°F oven or toaster oven. Preheat oven to broil. Set ovenproof soup bowls on a parchment-lined, rimmed baking sheet. Place 1 toasted round in the bottom of each bowl; ladle hot soup over round, filling nearly to the top. Lay desired number of cheese slices over soup, allowing cheese to overlap sides of bowl. Broil until cheese bubbles and is chestnut brown in spots. Watch closely: the cheese browns quickly. Serve immediately.

4 servings

BRAISED POT ROAST STEW

This is my rendition of a favorite family stew passed down from my grandmother to my mother and on to me. The aroma that wafts from our kitchen over the hours this stew is cooking is impossible to describe, but suffice it to say, no one is late for dinner. Better Feather Biscuits slathered with Better Butter (see Index for recipes) makes this comfort food meal complete.

about ½ cup unbleached all-purpose flour
1 pound chuck beef, cubed
1 teaspoon salt
several grindings of freshly ground black pepper
2 cups cubed white potatoes
1 cup sliced celery
1 cup chopped white onion
1 cup sliced carrots
3 garlic cloves, sliced
24 ounces vegetable juice
2 tablespoons quick-cooking tapioca

Preheat oven to 250°F. Place flour in a large bowl; coat beef cubes, covering all surfaces. Cover bottom of a cast-iron Dutch oven with canola oil and heat oil over moderately high heat. Transfer cubes of meat to cast-iron Dutch oven and brown meat on all sides. Remove from heat and season with salt and pepper. Add potatoes, celery, onion, carrots and garlic to beef cubes. Cover and set aside. In a medium bowl, mix tapioca with vegetable juice. Let mixture stand for about 15 minutes. Pour vegetable juice mixture over beef and vegetables and stir to combine. Cover and bake for 5 hours. Serve immediately.

6 servings

Recipe Overview

LIGHTER THAN HEARTY SOUPS

Cold Crab and Corn Soup

Golden Bisque with Pumpernickel Croutons

Gingered Coconut Carrot Soup

Lemon Yellow Zucchini Soup

Shrimp and Cucumber Bisque

A Bowl of Summer's Bounty

Summer's Harvest Soup

Curried Purslane Soup

Sunburst Squash Soup

ChickBanzo Chowder

Cold Zucchini Soup

Parsley and Potato Soup

Creamy Crab Soup

Asparagus Soup

Corn Chowder

Home-Harvested Gazpacho

COLD CRAB AND CORN SOUP

This soup is a pure representation of summer's bounty. Serve this refreshing and flavorful soup with a tossed green salad and good-quality bread. Prepare and cube the avocado just prior to serving.

4 cups buttermilk
¼ cup cooking sherry
1 tablespoon Dijon-style mustard
1 teaspoon salt
1 teaspoon Old Bay seasoning
1 pound crabmeat, picked of any shell
1½ cups cooked corn
½ cup minced fresh parsley
1 medium ripe avocado, cubed
1 large tomato, chopped (seeding is a matter of preference)

In a large bowl, whisk buttermilk with sherry, mustard, salt and Old Bay seasoning. Gently fold in crab, corn and parsley. Cover and refrigerate until ready to serve. Ladle soup into serving bowls and top with avocado cubes and chopped tomato.

6 servings

GOLDEN BISQUE WITH PUMPERNICKEL CROUTONS

The color of this bisque reminds me of glorious sunsets and autumn pumpkins. And the dark pumpernickel croutons contrast beautifully against the rich, mellow amber hue.

2 large red peppers, cut in half, stem and seeds removed
1 tablespoon olive oil
1 cup chopped onion
2 stalks celery, sliced
2 medium carrots, peeled and sliced
2 large potatoes (about 3½ cups), peeled and diced
4 cups chicken broth
1 teaspoon salt
several grindings of freshly ground black pepper
2½ cups cubed pumpernickel bread
olive oil, enough to lightly coat bread cubes
freshly grated Parmesan cheese

Set oven temperature to broil. Place pepper halves skin side up on a rimmed baking sheet and broil for 5–7 minutes or until skin is unevenly blackened. Remove from heat, cover the peppers and let stand for 20–30 minutes. When cool enough to handle, remove skin and coarsely chop. Heat olive oil in a large pot over medium-high heat, add onion and cook until slightly brown. Add chopped peppers, celery, carrots, potatoes, chicken broth and salt and pepper. Bring to a boil, cover, reduce heat and simmer for 20–25 minutes or until vegetables are fork-tender. In a food processor or blender, purée soup in batches; transfer puréed batches into a large bowl. Transfer all puréed soup back into original large pot and stir to blend. Simmer until heated through. Preheat oven to 350°F. In a large bowl, toss pumpernickel cubes with olive oil. Place on a parchment-lined rimmed baking sheet in a single layer and bake for 10–15 minutes or until crispy. Serve the soup hot and pass the pumpernickel croutons and Parmesan cheese to your guests.

8 servings

GINGERED COCONUT CARROT SOUP

This soup has that oh wow, jaw-dropping effect on people. It's my rendition of a delicious soup served by my friend, Joyce Kashima, one of the best hostesses I've ever had the pleasure of being entertained by. Serve Gingered Coconut Carrot Soup with Traditional Spinach Salad and Focaccia (see Index for recipes).

1 cup milk
1 cup water
1 vegetable bouillon cube
1 pound carrots, cut into chunks
1 white onion, cut into chunks (about 1 cup)
1½ teaspoons salt
1 teaspoon ground ginger
a dash of cayenne pepper
½ cup raw slivered almonds
1 can (14 ounces) coconut milk

In a large pot, combine milk, water and vegetable cube. Bring mixture to a boil over moderate heat. Add carrots, onion, salt, ginger, cayenne pepper and almonds. Cover, reduce heat to simmer (mixture should be rumbling) and cook for about 30–40 minutes or until the carrots are tender. Remove from heat and allow the mixture to cool slightly before transferring to a food processor or blender. Purée the carrot mixture in batches until silky smooth. Add coconut milk to the last batch to be puréed. Transfer all puréed soup back into original large pot and stir until well combined. Serve immediately.

6 servings

LEMON YELLOW ZUCCHINI SOUP

The first time I spotted bright orange zucchini look-alikes, I was at my local farmers market. I couldn't wait to get home and develop a recipe featuring them. The result is a beautiful, lemon-colored, velvety-smooth soup that makes for a memorable first course or light entrée. Orange zucchini is not very common, so if you can't find them locally, golden zucchini makes for an equally beautiful and delicious soup.

4–4½ cups sliced orange or golden zucchini
½ cup chopped white onion
4 tablespoons butter
1 cup milk
1 vegetable bouillon cube
a few grindings of freshly ground black pepper

Steam zucchini and onion in a large pot until fork-tender. Transfer to a food processor or blender, add butter and purée. Add milk, vegetable cube and pepper and purée until smooth. Transfer back into original pot and simmer until heated through. Serve immediately.

4 servings

SHRIMP AND CUCUMBER BISQUE

This is an unusual combination of ingredients that works with extraordinary results. The base of this bisque is velvety-smooth, making the bite-size morsels of shrimp a surprising contrast of textures. Serve with good-quality bread and a tossed salad.

6 tablespoons butter
2 cups chopped onion
6 tablespoons unbleached all-purpose flour
5 cups water
4 vegetable bouillon cubes
3 cups cucumber, peeled, seeded and cubed
1 cup milk
1 pound cooked shrimp, cut into bite-size pieces

Melt butter in a large pot over medium heat; add onion and sauté until tender. Gradually add flour, 1 tablespoon at a time, whisking after each addition. Gradually add water, 1 cup at a time, whisking after each addition. Add vegetable cubes and stir until cubes have dissolved into mixture. Add cucumbers, cover and bring mixture to a boil. Reduce heat and simmer until cucumbers are tender, about 10–15 minutes. Allow mixture to cool before transferring to a food processor or blender. Purée the cucumber mixture (in batches if necessary). Transfer all puréed mixture back into the original pot. Stir in milk and shrimp. Cook over low heat until heated through. Serve immediately.

8 servings

A BOWL OF SUMMER'S BOUNTY

When the Volvo Ocean Races (where yachts from all around the world compete) stopped in Baltimore's Inner Harbor, I was invited to do a cooking demonstration on the outdoor Chesapeake Bay cooking stage. I chose this particular soup because what could be more representative of Baltimore than Maryland crabs and Maryland corn and tomatoes? And what was the reaction of the crowd that sampled this soup? They gave me a standing ovation.

I recommend preparing this soup during the summer months, when crab is most plentiful and fresh corn can be scraped straight from the cob. To blanch and remove skin from tomatoes, cut an X on the bottom of the tomato, plunge into boiling water for 30 seconds, and remove using a slotted spoon. Allow the tomatoes to cool before coring and removing the skin.

2 tablespoons butter
1 cup chopped white onion
8–10 medium tomatoes, skins removed (seeding is a matter of preference)
1 cup heavy cream

In a large pot over moderate heat, melt butter and sauté onion and cook until tender. Add tomatoes and cook until they break down, about 10 minutes. Transfer mixture to a food processor or blender. Purée the mixture in batches until smooth. Add cream to the last batch and blend until fully incorporated. Return all puréed soup to the original pot and heat over moderate heat until hot.

1 pound crabmeat, picked of shell
½ cup fresh corn
1 tablespoon olive oil
1 teaspoon salt
freshly ground black pepper, to taste

In a medium bowl, gently toss crab, corn, olive oil, salt and pepper. Set aside or refrigerate until serving time.

BASIL OIL
3–4 garlic cloves
½ cup olive oil
1 teaspoon coarse salt
1 cup packed basil leaves

In a food processor, pulse garlic until chopped, add oil, salt and basil and pulse until basil leaves are chopped. Ladle soup into bowls. Pass the crab/corn mixture and Basil Oil to your guests.

6 servings

Summer's Harvest Soup

I was almost as wowed by the combination of flavors, colors and textures of this soup as my taste-testers were. As complementary accompaniments, I served with cold steamed shrimp and lump crabmeat. The seafood was passed around once the soup was served, and guests got to garnish their bowl with whatever they preferred.

When you're preparing the Basil Mixture, it's easier if you grate the lemon zest before you juice the lemon.

> *3 cups water*
> *2 vegetable bouillon cubes*
> *2 large, ripe summer tomatoes, chopped*
> *1 cup peeled, seeded and chopped cucumbers*
> *1 cup chopped yellow pepper*
> *1 cup fresh corn*
> *½ cup diagonally sliced celery*
> *½ cup thinly sliced sweet onions*
> *2 garlic cloves, minced*
> *½ teaspoon salt*
> *freshly ground black pepper, to taste*

In a medium pot, bring water to a boil, add vegetable cubes, and stir until the cubes have dissolved. Remove from heat and allow broth to cool before refrigerating. Refrigerate overnight.

In a large bowl (large enough to accommodate all ingredients including broth and basil mixture), toss tomatoes, cucumbers, yellow pepper, corn, celery, sweet onions and garlic; add salt and pepper to taste.

Basil Mixture
> *1 cup loosely packed basil leaves*
> *½ cup olive oil*
> *lemon zest from ½ of a lemon*
> *¼ cup lemon juice*
> *1 tablespoon cooking sherry*
> *½ teaspoon salt*
> *a few dashes Tabasco sauce or hot pepper sauce*

In a blender or food processor, combine basil leaves, olive oil, lemon zest, lemon juice, sherry, salt and Tabasco or hot pepper sauce. Blend until fully combined.

Add refrigerated vegetable broth to the vegetable mixture, stir in Basil Mixture and blend until evenly incorporated. Refrigerate until ready to serve.

8 servings

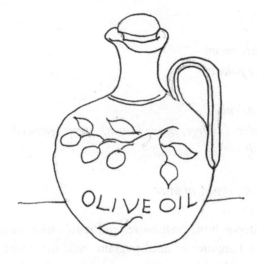

CURRIED PURSLANE SOUP

Purslane is a sprawling succulent plant with delicious edible green leaves that have a tangy, peppery flavor similar to arugula. It takes some time to remove the leaves from the stem, but it's well worth the effort; expect your guests to come back for seconds. Purslane is usually found at local farmers markets.

> *2 tablespoons butter*
> *1 cup chopped white onion*
> *2 tablespoons curry powder*
> *1 cup water*
> *1 vegetable bouillon cube*
> *8 cups purslane leaves (1 large, heavy bunch), stems removed*
> *1 cup half-and-half*
> *1 teaspoon salt*
> *freshly ground black pepper, to taste*

In a medium pot over moderate heat, melt butter and sauté onion until tender. Stir in curry powder and cook for about 1 minute or until fragrant. Add water and vegetable cube, bring mixture to a boil and add purslane leaves. Cover and simmer for about 15 minutes or until leaves are tender. Allow mixture to cool before transferring to a food processor or blender. Purée purslane mixture (in batches if necessary). Transfer all puréed purslane back into the original pot. Add half-and-half and salt; stir until well blended. Add pepper to taste. Serve immediately.

4 servings

Sunburst Squash Soup

I can't resist buying these vibrant yellow, scallop-edged "bursts of sunshine" when they arrive at my local farmers market. This is an elegant soup to serve as a first dinner course followed by Poached Cod on Lemon Beds and a tossed green salad. It also makes a lovely presentation as a luncheon entrée served with crusty bread and Leafy Greens with Radish and Eggs (see Index for recipes).

> *2 tablespoons butter*
> *1½ cups sliced white onions*
> *2 cups chicken broth*
> *4 medium sunburst squashes, unpeeled and sliced*
> *½ cup half-and-half*
> *1 teaspoon salt*
> *freshly ground black pepper, to taste*

Melt butter in a large pot over moderate heat and sauté onions until tender. Add chicken broth and squash. Cover and bring to a boil, reduce heat and simmer until squash is tender, about 10–15 minutes. Allow the squash mixture to cool before transferring to a food processor or blender. Purée in batches until velvety smooth; add half-and-half, and salt and pepper to the last batch to be puréed. As squash is puréed, transfer to a large bowl. After all squash mixture has been puréed, transfer back to original large pot. Stir until well blended and simmer until heated through. Serve immediately.

4 servings

ChickBanzo Chowder

A little playing around with the fact that chickpeas and garbanzo beans are one and the same and voilà! The word ChickBanzo was coined. (Better than GarPea Chowder, don't you think?) This colorful, nutritious, low-fat soup is full of texture and needs nothing more than a good, crispy bread to make it a memorable meal.

To blanch and remove skin from tomatoes, cut an X on the bottom of the tomato, plunge into boiling water for 30 seconds, and remove using a slotted spoon. Allow the tomatoes to cool before coring and removing skin.

>   *2 tablespoons olive oil*
>   *1 cup thinly sliced red onion*
>   *3 garlic cloves, minced*
>   *4 cups water*
>   *2 vegetable bouillon cubes*
>   *1 cup julienned carrots*
>   *2 large tomatoes, skins removed, coarsely chopped*
>   *10 ounces frozen spinach, defrosted, drained and squeezed dry*
>   *½ cup minced fresh parsley*
>   *1 can (14 ounces) chickpeas*
>   *freshly ground black pepper, to taste*

In a large pot, heat olive oil over moderate heat and sauté onion for about 2–3 minutes. Add garlic and sauté for another minute. Add water, vegetable cubes, carrots, tomatoes, cooked spinach, minced parsley and chickpeas. Cover, reduce heat to simmer and cook until carrots are fork-tender, about 5–10 minutes. Season the chowder with black pepper. Serve immediately.

6 servings

COLD ZUCCHINI SOUP

When the zucchini harvest is at its peak, I'm always looking for ways to use this prolific, delicately-flavored vegetable. Cold Zucchini Soup goes great with Tarragon Basil Chicken Salad (see page 162) and slices of juicy, summer tomatoes. As with any cold soup that has to be cooked first, plan accordingly, the soup needs to chill for several hours, or overnight, prior to serving.

> *2 tablespoons butter*
> *1 medium white onion, sliced*
> *2 cups chicken broth*
> *5 cups roughly chopped zucchini*
> *½ cup milk*
> *½ cup sour cream*
> *½ cup minced fresh parsley*
> *1 teaspoon salt*
> *freshly ground black pepper, to taste*
> *salsa (garnish)*

In a large pot over moderate heat, melt butter and sauté onion until tender. Add chicken broth and zucchini. Bring mixture to a boil, then lower heat to simmer. Cover and cook until zucchini is tender, about 5–10 minutes. Allow the mixture to cool slightly before transferring mixture to a food processor or blender. Purée zucchini mixture in batches until smooth; transfer puréed batches to a large bowl. Add milk, sour cream, parsley, salt and pepper to the final batch to be puréed. Transfer to the large bowl and stir until well blended. Refrigerate until well chilled. Ladle soup into bowls and serve with a dollop of salsa. Serve immediately.

4 servings

PARSLEY AND POTATO SOUP

This pale green soup with emerald flecks is a spin-off of vichyssoise, the cold potato and leek soup. Parsley and Potato Soup is lovely to serve as an entrée for lunch or as a first course before dinner. Potatoes come in several varieties, and my favorite for this soup is an all-purpose spud that's about golf ball size, has smooth skin and is buff-colored. This soup is best when made one day in advance, and it can be served either hot or cold.

> *2 tablespoons butter*
> *1 cup sliced white onions*
> *3 cups chicken broth*
> *8 golf ball size potatoes, unpeeled and quartered*
> *1 teaspoon salt*
> *1 cup milk*
> *1 bunch parsley, minced*

Melt butter in a large pot over moderate heat, add onions, and sauté until tender. Add chicken broth, potatoes and salt. Bring to a boil, cover and reduce heat and simmer for about 15 minutes or until potatoes are fork-tender. Allow mixture to cool slightly before transferring to a food processor or blender. Purée the soup (in batches if necessary) until velvety smooth. Add milk and parsley and pulse mixture a few times until ingredients are well blended. Transfer puréed mixture into a container and refrigerate overnight. Serve soup cold from the refrigerator or if you're serving it hot, bring the soup to room temperature before reheating. Simmer until hot and serve immediately.

6 servings

CREAMY CRAB SOUP

You'll often find more cream than crab in a spoonful of your everyday cream of crab soup. This rich-tasting soup is chock-full of crab, so much so that you may want to add an additional cup of broth to the recipe. For an elegant luncheon, serve Creamy Crab Soup as the main entrée with thin slices of Baked Ham (*This Book Cooks*), deviled eggs and slices of summer tomatoes. Taste the soup before seasoning with salt as ham broth can sometimes be salty. The ham broth produces a delicious pot of soup, but you can substitute chicken broth or vegetable broth with quite successful results.

> *6 tablespoons butter*
> *1 medium onion, finely chopped*
> *2 cups ham, chicken or vegetable broth*
> *2 cups heavy cream*
> *2 tablespoons cooking sherry*
> *½ cup minced fresh parsley*
> *2 pounds crabmeat, picked of any shell*
> *pepper, to taste*
> *salt (optional)*

In a large pot over moderate heat, melt butter and sauté onion until tender. Add broth and bring mixture to a boil. Reduce heat and add cream, sherry and parsley. Add crabmeat and stir until incorporated. Season the soup with pepper and salt, if desired. Serve immediately.

8 servings

ASPARAGUS SOUP

Asparagus is considered to be one of the most nutritionally well-balanced vegetables in existence, and when it's in season, it's high on my must-have list. If you're hosting a luncheon, this soup is perfectly complemented by Leafy Greens with Radish and Eggs and Free-Form Country Bread (see Index for recipes).

> *2 pounds fresh asparagus, ends trimmed*
> *4 tablespoons butter*
> *1 cup chopped white onion*
> *1 cup chopped celery*
> *4 tablespoons unbleached all-purpose flour*
> *2 cups chicken broth*
> *2 cups milk*
> *1 teaspoon salt*

Bring a large pot of water to a boil, drop in asparagus, and cook until tender but not mushy. Drain and set aside. In a large pot, melt butter over moderate heat. Add onion and celery, then sauté until tender. Lower heat and add flour, 1 tablespoon at a time, whisking after each addition. Slowly add chicken broth and whisk until smooth. Turn off heat, cover pot and let stand for about 15–20 minutes. Transfer cooked asparagus to a food processor or blender and pulse a few times. Add chicken broth mixture and purée until smooth. Add milk and salt and pulse until well blended. Return to large pot and simmer until heated through. Serve immediately.

6 servings

CORN CHOWDER

Every step of preparation for this delicious soup takes me back to my childhood summers spent in the kitchen with my grandmothers and mother. They spoke of the arrival of the corn harvest as though they were talking about a favorite friend or relative coming to visit for a summer holiday. Not only was corn going to be consumed straight from the cob, but together they were going to make corn fritters, creamed corn, corn pudding, corn cakes, cornbread and this all-time family favorite, Corn Chowder.

½ cup (1 stick) butter
1½ cups chopped white onion
½ cup chopped celery leaves
3 tablespoons unbleached all-purpose flour
2 cups water
2 vegetable bouillon cubes
5 cups corn (about 4–6 ears)
3 cups milk
1½ teaspoons salt
½ teaspoon paprika
freshly ground black pepper, to taste

In a large pot over medium heat, melt butter and sauté onion and celery leaves for about 3 minutes. Add flour 1 tablespoon at a time, whisking after each addition; flour will grab onion/celery mixture very quickly. Slowly add water, constantly stirring. Add vegetable cubes and stir until cubes have dissolved. Reduce heat to simmer. Roughly chop 2 cups of corn and add to the soup. Add remaining corn and milk and season with salt, paprika and pepper. Stir until fully incorporated. Serve hot.

8 servings

HOME-HARVESTED GAZPACHO

I have served many renditions of gazpacho over the years but this recipe ranks as one of my favorites. Gazpacho is a chilled, tomato-based, raw vegetable soup that originated in the south of Spain; some date it back to the Middle Ages. It has been referred to as liquid salad and as such is most flavorful during the summer when there's a bounty of fresh salad ingredients. Half of all the veggies in this recipe are puréed, giving this soup incredible body and texture.

To blanch and remove skin from tomatoes, cut an X on the bottom of the tomato, plunge into boiling water for 30 seconds, and remove using a slotted spoon. Allow tomatoes to cool before coring and removing skin.

2 large tomatoes, skins removed, seeded and cored
1 large cucumber, peeled, halved, seeds removed
1 medium onion, peeled and halved
1 green pepper, halved, seeded
3 cups vegetable or tomato juice
4 garlic cloves, minced
1 tablespoon olive oil
a few dashes Tabasco sauce or hot pepper sauce
¼ teaspoon salt
several grindings of freshly ground black pepper

In a food processor or blender, combine 1 tomato, ½ cucumber, ½ onion, ½ green pepper and 1 cup of the vegetable or tomato juice. Purée until well blended, then transfer to a large container. Chop the remaining tomato, cucumber, onion and green pepper. Add chopped vegetables and minced garlic to puréed mixture. Then add remaining 2 cups vegetable or tomato juice, olive oil, Tabasco or hot pepper sauce, salt and pepper. Stir until ingredients are incorporated. Cover and refrigerate overnight. Serve chilled.

6 servings

PESCATARIAN
Main Dishes

Here is a section devoted to pescatarians. This word is said to have derived from the Italian word for fish (*pesce*) combined with the ending of the English word, "vegetarian." I have no reason to believe this isn't true, since pescatarians are described as those who abstain from eating all meat and animal flesh with the exception of fish. Though not technically vegetarians (dairy and eggs are often included in this diet), more and more people are adopting this form of healthy eating while on their way to becoming full-fledged vegetarians. Many pescatarians believe that fish and/or fish oil is essential for optimum health because they are both quite high in omega-3 fatty acids. Full vegetarians use alternatives like flax seed oil to achieve these levels of omega-3 fatty acids.

Whether or not you're a pescatarian, this section is chock-full of kid-friendly, crowd-pleasing, unique recipes that range from perfect mid-week choices to casual or elegant weekend entertaining. Kids always love the Vegetable Lasagna and the Spinach, Tomato and Rice Pie. And you'll wow your grown-up guests with grown-up palates when you serve Seafood Macaroni and Cheese, Poached Cod on Lemon Beds, Lemon-Dressed Lobster Tails, Grilled Halloumi in a Bowl, or either of the two delicious crab dishes.

Many one-dish meals can also be found throughout this section—dishes that need nothing more than favored guests to partake of them. Other dishes offer suggestions for complementary sides. Whatever you choose to prepare, remember that when you choose to prepare it really does matter; always try to use ingredients at the peak of their harvest.

PESCATARIAN
Main Dishes

Crab Cakes

Anna's Pasta

Polenta Lasagna

Confetti Tuna Salad

Imperial Crab Imperial

A Feta Compli Spinach Pie

Lemon Pasta with Asparagus

Seafood Macaroni and Cheese

Poached Cod on Lemon Beds

Fresh Tomato and Cheddar Pie

Shrimp and Vegetable Quesadillas

Summer Rolls with Hoisin Peanut Sauce

Fusilli, Basil Brie and Summer Tomatoes

A Little Bit Farm/A Little Bit French Casserole

Asparagus and Shrimp with Grilled Halloumi

Cheddar Pie with Late Harvest Vegetables

Sweet Chili Peppers: Roasted and Stuffed

Roasted In-Season Vegetable Lasagna

Spinach, Tomato and Rice Pie

Lemon-Dressed Lobster Tails

Grilled Halloumi in a Bowl

Vegetable Lasagna

Soba Shrimp Salad

Greek-Style Shrimp

Summer Lasagna

Sesame Tofu

BanzoBurgers

CRAB CAKES

The crab industry has changed drastically over the years. Today, crabmeat comes from all over the world, and while imported crabmeat produces beautiful, large lumps, sometimes the meat can be tasteless. Consequently, the flavor of imported crabmeat varies greatly, leaving cooks to use their own judgment when seasoning. Domestic crabmeat is sweeter and includes the flavorful mustard that gives it a zestier flavor. So while both types of crabmeat work, I prefer domestic over imported.

1 egg
⅓ cup saltines or cracker crumbs (about 10 crackers)
¼ cup mayonnaise
1 tablespoon Dijon-style mustard
1 teaspoon Worcestershire sauce
1 tablespoon minced fresh parsley
1 pound lump crabmeat, picked of any shell
2 tablespoons butter

In a medium bowl, combine egg and saltines or cracker crumbs and whisk until combined. Let stand 5 minutes. Add mayonnaise, mustard, Worcestershire sauce and parsley and whisk until well blended. Gently fold in crabmeat. Divide mixture into 4 cakes. In a large skillet over medium heat, melt butter, turn heat to medium high, add crab cakes and cook until lightly brown on each side. Serve immediately.

4 crab cakes

ANNA'S PASTA

I had known my neighbor Anna for four years (the first four years of her life) when her parents decided to move to Ireland, the ancestral home of Anna's mom, Margaret. Anna, Margaret and I had become very good friends. Afternoons were often spent sipping tea and eating something wonderfully sweet that Margaret had whipped together for us. And many evenings found us partaking of delicious from-scratch Italian meals.

Fourteen years after moving away, Anna and her family planned a return trip to the states to celebrate her eighteenth birthday. The only gift Anna wanted from me was to have one of our wonderful lunches together: a cooked-from-scratch meal in our home. I prepared her favorite pasta dish and was thrilled when she said it was the best she had ever tasted. I made arrangements with the current owner of Anna's childhood home, and after lunch we visited it. Our luncheon reunion was as memorable and beautiful as Anna herself.

15 ounces whole milk ricotta cheese
2 tablespoons olive oil
1 teaspoon dried basil
2 teaspoons salt
several grindings of freshly ground black pepper
1 pound ziti, cooked according to package directions

In a large bowl, combine ricotta cheese, olive oil, basil, salt and pepper. Add pasta and toss to coat evenly. Adjust olive oil, basil, salt and pepper seasonings if necessary. Serve immediately.

6 to 8 servings

POLENTA LASAGNA

Polenta reigns supreme in northern Italy; it's even more popular than pasta. In this lasagna recipe, layers of cheese, vegetables and polenta have been described as "exquisite comfort food."

1 tablespoon olive oil
1 package (8 ounces) white mushrooms, sliced
1½ cups tomato sauce
16 ounces polenta, cut into 16 slices
½ cup shredded carrots
8 ounces mozzarella cheese, cut into about 16 slices
½ cup freshly grated Parmesan cheese
¼ cup minced fresh parsley

Preheat oven to 350°F. Heat olive oil in a medium skillet over moderate heat and sauté mushrooms until tender. Spread ¾ cup tomato sauce in the bottom of a 13 x 9-inch baking dish that has been lightly oiled with cooking spray. Top the sauce with the sautéed mushrooms and 8 slices of the polenta. Top the polenta with shredded carrots, 8 mozzarella slices and ¼ cup of the Parmesan cheese. Top the Parmesan cheese with remaining ¾ cup tomato sauce and cover tomato sauce with remaining 8 slices of polenta. Top the polenta with the remaining ¼ cup of Parmesan cheese and parsley. Cover and bake for 30 minutes. Remove cover, switch oven setting to broil and brown top. Serve immediately.

6 to 8 servings

CONFETTI TUNA SALAD

When my brother Kraig and I were kids, he used to make the best tasting tuna fish salad. It varied with each preparation, but no matter what he combined, it always tasted so good. This is my rendition, which includes many of the ingredients I remember him using. I particularly like the variety of colors and the addition of hard-boiled eggs; they give the tuna great texture. Serve as a sandwich or on a bed of lettuce with crispy crackers.

12 ounces solid white albacore tuna, packed in water, drained
2 hard-boiled eggs, chopped
⅓ cup finely chopped carrot
⅓ cup finely chopped celery
⅓ cup finely chopped red and/or yellow pepper
⅓ cup minced red onion
2 tablespoons minced fresh parsley
about ½ cup mayonnaise or more
freshly ground black pepper, to taste

In a large bowl, break tuna apart with a fork. Add eggs, carrots, celery, red and/or yellow pepper, onion, parsley, mayonnaise and black pepper. Mix until mayonnaise is distributed evenly. Serve immediately or refrigerate until serving time.

6 servings

IMPERIAL CRAB IMPERIAL

This is an elegant dish, and great if you're hosting an important dinner.

2 eggs
¼ cup saltines or cracker crumbs (about 7–8 crackers)
1 teaspoon dry mustard
1 teaspoon salt
1 teaspoon Worcestershire sauce
⅓ cup minced red pepper
1 pound lump crabmeat, picked of any shell
½ cup mayonnaise, more or less based on your preference

Preheat oven to 350°F. In a large bowl, lightly beat eggs and add saltines or cracker crumbs, dry mustard, salt, Worcestershire sauce and minced red pepper. Fold in crabmeat. Divide mixture evenly into four individual baking shells or ramekins. Top desired amount of mayonnaise over crab. Bake for about 15–20 minutes or until crab is heated through. Place under broiler to lightly brown the top. Serve immediately.

4 servings

A FETA COMPLI SPINACH PIE

The sweet flavor of caramelized onions combined with the tanginess of feta cheese results in this incredibly tasty pie.

> *2 tablespoons olive oil*
> *3 medium onions (about 3 cups), thinly sliced*
> *1 teaspoon sugar*
> *½ teaspoon salt*
> *10 ounces frozen chopped spinach,* defrosted, drained, and squeezed dry
> *1 cup milk*
> *6 eggs*
> *1¼ cups crumbled feta cheese*

Preheat oven to 350°F. Lightly oil a 9-inch pie plate with cooking spray. In a sauté pan, heat olive oil over moderate heat. Add onions, sugar and salt. Cook for about 20–30 minutes, stirring occasionally until golden brown. Remove from heat. Arrange spinach in bottom of pie plate and top with sautéed onions. In a large bowl, whisk milk and eggs until well combined and then pour egg mixture over onions. Top pie with crumbled feta and bake for about 50 minutes or until knife inserted in center of pie comes out clean. Serve immediately.

6 to 8 servings

Lemon Pasta with Asparagus

This recipe is a delicious and colorful representation of spring. And it's simple to assemble. Serve with a tossed green salad and crusty bread. I prefer to break the angel hair pasta in half because I think the ingredients are easier to incorporate. The thickness of asparagus spears is a matter of preference and will determine the amount of cooking time; I prefer medium size spears. It's easier if you grate the lemon zest before you juice the lemon.

2 eggs
1 cup milk
8 ounces angel hair pasta
1 bunch fresh asparagus, trimmed and cut into 1-inch diagonal pieces
3 tablespoons butter
2 teaspoons grated lemon zest
3 tablespoons fresh lemon juice
½ teaspoon salt
freshly grated Parmesan cheese

In a medium bowl, whisk eggs and milk until well combined. Set aside. In a large pot, cook pasta in salted, boiling water for about 4 minutes. Add asparagus pieces to the pasta and cook an additional 2–3 minutes or until asparagus is just fork-tender. Remove from heat and drain pasta and asparagus. Return the mixture to the pot and cover. Melt butter in a medium skillet over moderate heat and add grated lemon zest, lemon juice and salt. Cook for about 1 minute. Pour lemon/butter mixture over pasta/asparagus and toss. Add egg/milk mixture to pasta/asparagus combination and cook over low heat for a few minutes or until mixture slightly thickens, stirring constantly. Serve immediately with freshly grated Parmesan cheese.

4 to 6 servings

SEAFOOD MACARONI AND CHEESE

Catering clients Luke and Marina Cooper asked me to prepare seafood macaroni and cheese for a party they were hosting. I'd never made or eaten the dish, but it only took one test batch to convince me that this was a winning mixture of ingredients and an exciting new dish. Seafood Macaroni and Cheese takes time to assemble, but I think you'll agree that the results will be more than worth your effort. Serve it alone or accompanied by a leafy green salad, your favorite tomato dish or any of the tomato dishes in my first cookbook, *This Book Cooks*.

Crawfish meat (the seafood used in this recipe) is pre-cooked and can be found in the frozen section of the seafood department in most grocery stores. Crawfish meat takes about 2–2½ hours (sometimes longer) to thaw.

16 ounces or 1 pound elbow macaroni
2 vegetable bouillon cubes
8 ounces light cream cheese, softened
32 ounces cream
1 tablespoon cooking sherry
16 ounces or 1 pound crawfish meat, thawed
2 cups shredded cheddar cheese
2 cups shredded Swiss cheese
freshly ground black pepper
2 tablespoons butter
1 cup soft bread cubes
½ cup grated fresh Parmesan cheese

In a large pot, cook macaroni according to package directions. Drain pasta and return to pot. Add vegetable cubes and cream cheese to pasta pot. Cover and let stand for about 5–7 minutes or until cream cheese has melted slightly. Preheat oven to 350°F. Add one container of cream and stir pasta until ingredients are incorporated. Add remaining container of cream, sherry, crawfish meat, cheddar cheese and 1 cup of Swiss cheese. Season the mixture with black pepper and stir until well combined. Transfer mixture to a lightly oiled 4-quart baking dish.

In a small pan, melt butter and toss the bread cubes with the butter. Top baking dish with bread cubes, remaining cup of Swiss cheese and the Parmesan cheese. Bake uncovered for about 20–30 minutes or until bread cubes are lightly browned and macaroni and cheese is bubbling. Serve immediately.

12 to 14 servings

POACHED COD ON LEMON BEDS

This is an entrée my husband has dubbed, "Invite-friends-for-dinner." The ingredients are among some of my favorite foods, not to mention their healthy reputation: cod, olive oil, lemon and fresh parsley. It's simple to assemble, elegant and most impressive to serve. The flavor of the poached cod speaks for itself, so the choice of sides doesn't need to be overly embellished. Slices of summer tomatoes, a tossed green salad, boiled new potatoes, steamed green beans, rice or sautéed zucchini round out this dish beautifully.

3 lemons, thinly sliced, seeds removed (about 24 slices)
2 pounds fresh cod fillets (4 pieces, ½-inch thick), skin removed
1½ teaspoons salt
freshly ground black pepper
¼ cup capers, drained
⅓ cup minced fresh parsley
1 cup extra virgin olive oil

Preheat oven to 250°F. Arrange 12 lemon slices in the bottom of a 15 x 10-inch baking dish (4-quart capacity) and top the lemon slices with cod fillets. Sprinkle with salt and pepper. Distribute capers and parsley evenly over fillets. Top the fillets with remaining slices of lemon. Pour olive oil evenly over lemon slices and bake uncovered for 1 hour. Serve immediately.

4 servings

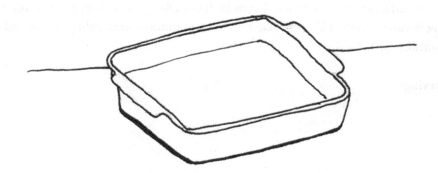

FRESH TOMATO AND CHEDDAR PIE

Back in the 1940s, Nick's mother took a road trip to California. Upon her return to Baltimore, she described the highlight of her trip as eating an incredible fresh tomato pie, one of the best things she had ever eaten. She raved so much about this pie that eventually the whole family traveled to the west coast—just for the pie! This fabulous tomato pie was the precursor to one of our most popular dishes, the Pizza Pie. Prepare User-Friendly Pie Crust (see page 47), or if crunched for time, buy a good frozen 9-inch pie shell.

½ cup mayonnaise
1 cup shredded cheddar cheese
2 tablespoons white wine
½ teaspoon dry mustard
¼ teaspoon cracked black pepper
½ teaspoon garlic powder
½ teaspoon salt
2 tablespoons minced fresh parsley
1 pie shell (9 inches), baked according to directions
3–4 medium tomatoes, sliced (enough to fill the pie nearly ¾ full)
about 15–20 fresh basil leaves

Preheat oven to 350°F. In a medium bowl, combine mayonnaise, ½ cup cheddar cheese, white wine, dry mustard, black pepper, garlic powder, salt and parsley; mix until incorporated. Arrange half of the tomatoes in the baked pie shell and top with fresh basil leaves. Top basil leaves with remaining tomato slices. Dollop the cheddar/mayonnaise mixture over the tomatoes. Don't worry about perfection; the mixture will even itself out during the baking process. Top with the remaining ½ cup of cheddar cheese. Bake for 35–45 minutes or until lightly brown and bubbly. Serve immediately.

4 to 6 servings

SHRIMP AND VEGETABLE QUESADILLAS

If you have a counter-service-style kitchen and are feeding family or entertaining friends for an informal dinner, this recipe is a good choice because the quesadillas are best eaten immediately after they're prepared.

1 tablespoon olive oil
1 garlic clove, minced
1 cup chopped white onion
1 cup fresh corn
1 cup chopped tomatoes
a few dashes Tabasco sauce or hot pepper sauce
½ pound medium shrimp, cooked, peeled, deveined and chopped
2 tablespoons fresh lemon juice
¼ teaspoon salt
4 flour tortillas (4 inches)
1 cup shredded mozzarella cheese
1–2 avocados, cut into chunks
salsa

Heat 1 tablespoon olive oil in a large skillet over moderate heat and sauté garlic and onion for 1–2 minutes. Add corn, tomatoes and Tabasco or hot pepper sauce and sauté an additional 3–4 minutes. Stir in shrimp, lemon juice and salt, and cook until heated through. Reduce heat to low and cover to keep warm. In another skillet that will accommodate the full size of a tortilla, heat 1 tablespoon olive oil over medium-high heat. Place tortilla in skillet and top half of the tortilla with ¼ cup mozzarella and ½ cup vegetable/shrimp mixture. Fold tortilla over and cook for 1–2 minutes on each side or until lightly browned. Repeat this process with remaining tortillas, adding about 1 tablespoon olive oil to the skillet for each quesadilla. Serve immediately and pass the avocado and salsa to your guests.

4 servings

SUMMER ROLLS WITH HOISIN PEANUT SAUCE

I love preparing these Summer Rolls on hot, humid summer nights when the only food I want to eat is cold, refreshing and not too filling. Rice paper and hoisin sauce can be found in the international section of most grocery stores. Rice paper is particularly thin and at first can be challenging to work with, but once you get the hang of it, you'll be rolling like a pro. These rolls can be assembled in advance; arrange them on a platter in a single layer, making sure that the rolls don't touch one another, because they'll stick together. When buying mung bean sprouts look for plump, white sprouts; for optimum freshness, they should be purchased the day you plan to make the rolls.

HOISIN PEANUT SAUCE

¼ cup natural peanut butter
¼ cup water
2 tablespoons hoisin sauce
1 tablespoon toasted sesame oil
1 tablespoon tamari or low sodium soy sauce

In a small bowl, combine peanut butter, water, hoisin sauce, sesame oil and tamari or soy sauce. Whisk until well blended. Set aside.

8 rice paper wrappers (8½-inch diameter wrappers)
8 large cooked shrimp, cut in half lengthwise
16 large fresh basil leaves
1 cucumber, peeled, cut into 3 x ½-inch sticks (16 sticks)
1 large ripe avocado, sliced (16 slices)
about 2 cups mung bean sprouts

In a shallow dish that accommodates the rice paper wrapper (a pie plate works well) soak 1 sheet of rice paper in hot water for 3 seconds or until soft and pliable. Transfer to a cutting board. Lay 2 halves of a shrimp, cut side up, in the center of the paper, top shrimp with 2 basil leaves, top basil leaves with 2 cucumber sticks, 2 slices of avocado and several mung bean sprouts. Fold each side of rice paper toward center, take the bottom half of paper and fold over filling, roll to close. Serve immediately with Hoisin Peanut Sauce or cover and refrigerate until serving time.

4 servings

FUSILLI, BASIL BRIE AND SUMMER TOMATOES

When summer tomatoes are at the height of their growing season, I love to prepare this flavorful and colorful one-dish entrée.

3 cups basil leaves
½ cup olive oil
¼ cup seasoned rice vinegar
½ teaspoon salt
several grindings of freshly ground black pepper
½ pound Brie, cut into bite-size pieces
½ pound fusilli (3 cups dry measure)
2 medium tomatoes, cut into bite-size pieces

In a blender or food processor, combine basil leaves, olive oil, vinegar, salt and pepper to taste. Process until incorporated. Place Brie in a small bowl and toss with the basil marinade. Refrigerate for a few hours. Cook fusilli according to package directions; drain and transfer to a large bowl. Toss pasta with tomatoes. Add marinated Brie to pasta and tomatoes. Toss until well combined. Divide evenly into 6 shallow serving bowls. Serve immediately.

6 servings

A LITTLE BIT FARM/A LITTLE BIT FRENCH CASSEROLE

The first time I made this, my husband and I could hardly control ourselves from eating the entire casserole at one sitting. It's a fresh-tasting, colorful, summer-comfort-food dish that's as great to serve for breakfast as it is for lunch or dinner.

½ cup half-and-half
1 teaspoon Dijon-style mustard
1 teaspoon Herbes de Provence
1 teaspoon salt
a dash of cayenne pepper
8 eggs
1 cup shredded zucchini
1 medium tomato, chopped
3 cups shredded cheddar cheese

Preheat oven to 350°F. In a large bowl, combine half-and-half, mustard, Herbes de Provence, salt and cayenne pepper. Whisk in eggs, add zucchini, tomato, and 2 cups of cheese. Stir until well blended. Lightly oil a 9-inch baking dish with cooking spray. Pour mixture into dish and top with remaining cup of cheese. Bake for 45 minutes or until a knife inserted in the center comes out clean. Serve immediately.

6 servings

ASPARAGUS AND SHRIMP WITH GRILLED HALLOUMI

Halloumi ranks as one of my all-time favorite cheeses because of its wonderful flavor and texture. And who wouldn't marvel at a cheese that can be sautéed or grilled yet still keeps its shape and doesn't melt? On the day I first tried this recipe, my sister was dropping off her two Norwich terriers for an overnight visit, and she and a friend arrived just in time for the taste-testing. They loved my creation, and I liked it so much that I submitted the recipe to the Features Editor of the *Examiner*, who promptly published it.

1 pound large shrimp, cooked, peeled and deveined
3 tablespoons olive oil
2 tablespoons fresh lemon juice
½ teaspoon salt
several grindings of freshly ground black pepper
1 bunch fresh asparagus, trimmed and cut into bite-size pieces
1 tablespoon olive oil
½ pound halloumi cheese, cubed
2 tablespoons toasted sunflower seeds

In a medium bowl, combine shrimp with 3 tablespoons olive oil, lemon juice, salt and black pepper. Marinate for 3 hours. Cook asparagus in rumbling water for 3–5 minutes or until desired tenderness; for best results, asparagus should be tender crisp. Run asparagus under cold water, or let them sit in an ice bath until cooled. Heat 1 tablespoon olive oil in a medium skillet over moderate heat, add halloumi cubes and sauté for about 2 minutes or until just slightly brown. Place 4–5 shrimp into each of 6 rimmed serving bowls. Top the shrimp with asparagus pieces and cubes of halloumi cheese. Spoon reserved marinade over the ingredients, distributing evenly and top with toasted sunflower seeds. Serve immediately.

6 servings

CHEDDAR PIE WITH
LATE HARVEST VEGETABLES

For me, this beautiful Cheddar Pie, hot from the oven, is the quintessential comfort food, as well as a perfect base dish for eating foods in-season. Almost any fresh, seasonal food can find its way into the filling. Prepare this dish when peppers and tomatoes are at the height of their growing season. You will need 1 cup of Roasted In-Season Vegetables (see page 51) for the recipe. I prefer homemade pie crust, but if you don't have the time or the inclination, buy a good quality frozen pie shell.

> 1⅛ cup unbleached all-purpose flour
> ½ teaspoon salt
> ¼ cup olive oil
> 2½–3 tablespoons cold water
> 8 eggs
> ½ cup heavy cream
> ½ teaspoon salt
> a dash of cayenne pepper
> 1 tablespoon Dijon-style mustard
> 3 cups freshly grated cheddar cheese
> 1 cup Roasted In-Season Vegetables

In a medium bowl, combine flour and salt. Drizzle olive oil over flour and toss until flour mixture is coarse. Slowly drizzle in cold water. Knead dough a few times to fully incorporate ingredients. Add more water if dough doesn't come together or seems dry. Let dough rest for a few minutes. Lightly flour work surface and roll the dough until it is about 12 inches in diameter. (If dough begins to resist, let it rest for a few minutes.) Transfer to a 9-inch pie plate and flute edges. Preheat oven to 350°F. In a large bowl, beat eggs with a wire whisk; add cream, salt and cayenne pepper. Spread mustard evenly over the bottom and sides of unbaked pie crust. Sprinkle 1 cup of cheese over mustard. Top the cheese with roasted vegetables and top the vegetables with 1 cup of the cheese. Pour egg mixture over cheese and top pie with remaining cup of cheese. Bake for 45 minutes or until lightly brown and knife inserted in center comes out clean. Allow the pie to cool for about 10 minutes before serving.

6 servings

SWEET CHILI PEPPERS: ROASTED AND STUFFED

When sweet chili peppers are at the peak of their growing season, this dish is on my list of must-haves. When it comes to selecting sweet chili peppers, choose from Italian, Anaheim (California green) or poblano peppers. I like to serve this with a salsa that has the addition of beans and corn or serve it with your favorite salsa.

>*2 medium ripe avocados, halved and pitted, reserve 1 pit*
>*2 garlic cloves, minced*
>*2 tablespoons fresh lime juice*
>*salt, to taste*
>*6 mild chili peppers, halved lengthwise, seeds and stems removed*
>*¼ cup chèvre cheese*
>*1 cup shredded Jarlsberg cheese*
>*½ cup shredded mozzarella cheese*
>*salsa*

In a medium bowl, mash avocado. Stir in garlic, lime juice and salt. Add reserved pit (to prevent browning) and cover. Let stand at room temperature until ready to serve. Remove pit just before serving.

Set oven to broil. Place peppers on a parchment-lined baking sheet, skin side up; broil until charred. Place peppers in a paper bag. Loosely close bag. Let peppers cool in bag for about 5 minutes. Remove skin from peppers. In a medium bowl, combine chèvre, Jarlsberg and mozzarella cheeses. Stuff peppers with cheese mixture and place on baking sheet. Broil for 5–7 minutes or until cheese is melted and slightly browned. Serve immediately with seasoned avocado mixture and salsa.

6 servings

ROASTED IN-SEASON VEGETABLE LASAGNA

Roasted In-Season Vegetables give this lasagna a rich, earthy flavor. Serve with authentic Italian bread for a comfort food meal you won't soon forget. You will need 3 cups of Roasted In-Season Vegetables (see page 51) for the recipe.

15 ounces ricotta cheese
1 egg
½ cup minced fresh parsley
several grindings of freshly ground black pepper
25 ounces marinara sauce
9 lasagna noodles, uncooked
3 cups Roasted In-Season Vegetables
1 pound fresh mozzarella cheese, sliced into 27 slices
¾ cup freshly grated Parmesan cheese

Preheat oven to 350°F. In a medium bowl, combine ricotta, egg, parsley and pepper. Mix until ingredients are fully incorporated. In a 13 x 9-inch pan, spread 1 cup of marinara sauce evenly along the bottom of the pan and top the sauce with 3 lasagna noodles. Spread about 1 cup of the ricotta mixture over noodles; don't worry about being perfect, the ricotta will even out during cooking. Top the ricotta with 1 cup of the vegetables, 9 slices of mozzarella cheese and ¼ cup Parmesan cheese. Repeat layering with 1 cup sauce, 3 lasagna noodles, remaining ricotta mixture, 1 cup vegetables, 9 slices mozzarella cheese and ¼ cup Parmesan. Top with remaining noodles, vegetables, mozzarella, marinara sauce, and Parmesan cheese. Cover and bake lasagna for 45 minutes. Remove cover and bake an additional 15 minutes. Let lasagna stand for about 10–15 minutes before serving.

8 to 10 servings

SPINACH, TOMATO AND RICE PIE

Working with one of my favorite food combinations—spinach and tomatoes—and a few containers of leftover rice from an evening of Chinese carry-out, I created this comfort food pie. Complementary sides are Herb-Dressed Cabbage Salad or Apple Celery Salad with Peanut Vinaigrette (see Index for recipes).

3 cups cooked white rice
2 eggs
1 cup heavy cream
1½ cups chopped fresh tomatoes
10 ounces frozen spinach, defrosted, drained and squeezed dry
½ cup shredded carrots
1 cup crumbled feta cheese
½ teaspoon salt
several grindings of freshly ground black pepper

Preheat oven to 350°F. In a large bowl, combine rice, eggs and cream. Fold in tomatoes, spinach, carrots, feta cheese, salt and pepper. Transfer to a 9-inch pie dish and bake for about 35–45 minutes or until light brown and bubbly. Serve immediately.

6 servings

LEMON-DRESSED LOBSTER TAILS

This lemony dressing is a perfect complement to the succulent flavor of lobster. Serve with baked potatoes and Spinach Gratin (see page 191).

½ cup fresh lemon juice (about 3–4 lemons)
¼ cup canola oil
1 tablespoon rice vinegar
4–5 drops Tabasco sauce or hot pepper sauce
1 garlic clove, crushed
1 tablespoon dry mustard
1 tablespoon salt
6 lobster tails (7 to 8 ounces each)
melted butter

In a medium bowl, mix lemon juice, oil, vinegar, Tabasco or hot pepper sauce and garlic. Whisk until fully combined. Whisk in mustard and salt. Set oven to broil (high broil if you have the option). Remove lobster fins, and with a sharp knife, make an incision on the underside of the lobster, starting from the top and working down to the tail. Steam partially frozen lobster in a single layer for 4 minutes. If you don't have a pot large enough to accommodate the 6 tails, steam in batches or use two pots. Transfer lobster tails to a baking sheet that has been lined with parchment paper. Spoon half of the dressing over the underside of each tail and broil for 2 minutes. Turn lobsters over, spoon remaining dressing over each tail and broil for an additional 2 minutes. Serve immediately with melted butter.

6 servings

GRILLED HALLOUMI IN A BOWL

This idea came to me while on assignment, trying to think of unique ways to serve grilled cheese sandwiches; more specifically, grilled halloumi cheese sandwiches. From my fond childhood memories of dipping orange-centered grilled cheese sandwiches into smooth-as-cream tomato soup with my grandmother, this fabulous recipe came into being. Halloumi (the traditional cheese of Cyprus) doesn't melt when it's heated. It's salty, so if you're sensitive to salt, reduce the amount to ½ teaspoon or simply salt to taste.

>   *2 tablespoons canola oil*
>   *1 cup chopped white onion*
>   *2 garlic cloves, finely minced*
>   *2 cans (28 ounces each) diced tomatoes*
>   *⅛ cup sugar*
>   *1 teaspoon oregano*
>   *1 teaspoon basil*
>   *½–1 teaspoon salt (optional)*
>   *¼–½ teaspoon red pepper flakes*
>   *several grindings of freshly ground black pepper*
>   *2 packages (8.8 ounces each) halloumi cheese*
>   *8 slices (½-inch each) ciabatta bread*

Heat canola oil in a large pot over moderate heat; add onion and garlic and sauté until tender. Add tomatoes, sugar, oregano, basil, salt, red pepper flakes and black pepper. Reduce heat to simmer and cook uncovered for about ½ hour or longer. Cut each brick of halloumi into 8 slices. Cover the bottom of a large skillet with canola oil. Over moderate heat, sauté halloumi (in batches) about 1–2 minutes on each side until light golden brown (browning is usually uneven). Transfer cheese to a platter. To grill the bread, cover the bottom of skillet with oil. Over moderately high heat, add slices of bread (in batches) and grill bread on each side until golden. Transfer bread slices into 8 shallow bowls and top each slice with a ladleful of seasoned tomatoes. Top each bowl with two slices of halloumi cheese. Serve immediately.

8 servings

VEGETABLE LASAGNA

In my rendition of vegetable lasagna, raw moisture-rich shredded carrots and zucchini are added for their fiber content and nutrients, as well as for color. Because it has no prior cooking requirements, I assembled this dish in less than 30 minutes.

15 ounces ricotta cheese
1 cup shredded carrots
1 cup shredded zucchini
½ teaspoon salt
freshly ground black pepper
2½ cups tomato sauce
6 pieces no-boil (also called oven ready) lasagna noodles
8 ounces mozzarella cheese, shredded
¼ cup freshly grated Parmesan cheese

Preheat oven to 350°F. In a medium bowl, combine ricotta cheese, carrots, zucchini, salt and pepper. Spread 1 cup tomato sauce in the bottom of an 11 x 7-inch baking dish. Place 2 uncooked noodles over the sauce, side by side. Spread half of the ricotta mixture over noodles. Evenly distribute half of the mozzarella cheese over ricotta mixture. Top mozzarella with two lasagna noodles, spoon 1 cup sauce over noodles, spread remaining ricotta mixture over sauce. Place remaining two noodles over ricotta, spread a thin layer of remaining tomato sauce over noodles, top with remaining mozzarella and sprinkle with grated Parmesan. Cover and bake for 45 minutes or until bubbly. Remove cover, set oven temperature to broil, and lightly brown the top. Allow the lasagna to cool for about 15 minutes before serving.

6 servings

SOBA SHRIMP SALAD

With an abundance of color, flavor and texture, this cold, main-dish salad receives rave reviews every time I serve it. There are several variations of soba noodles, I use Eden Foods Wild Yam Soba.

2 teaspoons salt
¼ teaspoon black pepper
2 teaspoons Dijon-style mustard
½ cup apple cider vinegar
1½ cups extra virgin olive oil
2 packages (8.8 ounces each) soba noodles, broken in half
1½ pounds steamed jumbo shrimp, peeled, deveined
1 cup frozen peas, thawed
1 cup yellow pepper, cut into ½-inch pieces
1 cup orange pepper, cut into ½-inch pieces
1 can (14 ounces) artichoke hearts in water, drained and quartered
½ cup pitted, roughly chopped Kalamata olives
½ cup sliced green onions
1 cup crumbled feta cheese
1 cup cherry tomatoes, cut in half

In a 3–4 cup jar with a tight-fitting lid, combine salt, pepper, mustard and apple cider vinegar. Cover and shake mixture vigorously. Add olive oil, cover and shake until ingredients are incorporated. Keep dressing at room temperature until ready to use. Cook noodles according to package directions. Cool to room temperature. In a large bowl, combine shrimp, peas, yellow pepper, orange pepper, artichoke hearts, olives and green onions. Toss with just enough dressing to lightly coat the ingredients. Toss noodles with the remaining dressing or just enough to evenly coat the pasta. Transfer the noodles to a large shallow serving bowl and toss them with the shrimp and vegetables. Top the salad with crumbled feta cheese and cherry tomatoes. Serve immediately.

10 to 12 servings

GREEK-STYLE SHRIMP

This is a colorful and nutritious one-dish entrée that won't disappoint. It takes time to assemble, mostly because the rice and shrimp have to be cooked prior to assembling. For the rice, I like to use a combination of long grain rice and wild rice.

1 cup Greek yogurt
2 tablespoons olive oil
1 teaspoon oregano
½ teaspoon red pepper flakes or to taste
½ cup pitted and chopped Kalamata olives
16 ounces frozen spinach, defrosted, drained and squeezed dry
2 cans (14.5 ounces) diced tomatoes
1 can (15 ounces) garbanzo beans, drained
1½ cups cooked rice
1 bag (16 ounces) large shrimp, cooked, peeled and deveined
2 tablespoons olive oil
zest from one lemon
1 teaspoon salt
½ cup minced parsley
1 cup feta cheese

In a medium bowl, combine yogurt with olive oil, oregano, red pepper flakes and Kalamata olives. Stir until well blended. Refrigerate until serving time. Preheat oven to 350°F. Place spinach in a 13 x 9-inch glass baking dish. Top spinach with 1 can of tomatoes. Top tomatoes with the garbanzo beans and evenly distribute the rice over the beans. In a medium bowl, toss shrimp with olive oil, lemon zest and salt. Top beans with shrimp, arranging shrimp in a single layer. Top shrimp with remaining can of tomatoes and sprinkle parsley over tomatoes. Evenly distribute feta cheese over tomatoes. Cover and bake for 20–30 minutes or until heated through and bubbly. Serve immediately and pass the yogurt mixture to your guests.

8 servings

SESAME TOFU

Tofu's lack of any distinguishable flavor allows for the addition of intense taste enhancements like the abundantly flavored sauce in this recipe. The outstanding properties of this dish are not only the delicious sauce, but also the combination of my favorite textures: crispy on the outside and soft on the inside. I like to serve this dish with steamed rice.

2 packages (14 ounces each) extra firm tofu
⅓ cup honey
¼ cup tamari
2 tablespoons toasted sesame oil
2 tablespoons brown rice vinegar
2 cloves garlic, minced
1 teaspoon powdered ginger
½ teaspoon red pepper flakes
cornstarch
½ cup canola oil
⅛ cup toasted sesame seeds
1 cup frozen peas, thawed
½ cup roasted and salted peanuts

Place the tofu on a plate and top the tofu with another plate. Top the plate with a cast-iron skillet or a weighted casserole dish, pan or platter. Allow the tofu to drain for 30 minutes or longer. In a medium saucepan, combine honey, tamari, sesame oil, vinegar, garlic, powdered ginger and red pepper flakes and mix until well blended. Heat the sauce over moderate heat. Cut each tofu block into 6 slices, cut each slice in half, cut each half on the diagonal to form a triangle. Place triangles in a shallow, rimmed vessel. Evenly distribute cornstarch over tofu, gently covering all surfaces; a flour sifter works great. Heat oil in a sauté pan over moderately high heat. Add tofu and cook in batches until golden brown on all surfaces. Transfer tofu to a shallow serving dish to accommodate and gently toss with sauce. Top with toasted sesame seeds, peas and peanuts. Serve immediately.

6 to 8 servings

SUMMER LASAGNA

I had been daydreaming about making a fresh vegetable lasagna all summer. I was thrilled with the results of my daydreaming, as was Nick. You need nothing more to complete this meal than good-quality Italian bread and olive oil for dipping. Use a combination of both red and yellow tomatoes; a different color for each layer makes a beautiful presentation. Don't be alarmed when you remove the lasagna from the oven and it looks like it's swimming in liquid; fresh vegetables naturally produce this liquid during the cooking process.

2 eggs
15 ounces ricotta cheese
½ cup freshly grated Parmesan cheese
½ cup minced fresh parsley
1 teaspoon salt
several grindings of freshly ground black pepper
4–6 medium red and/or yellow tomatoes, sliced
1 additional tomato, chopped, for top of lasagna
about 2 cups fresh basil leaves
6 pieces no-boil (also called oven ready) lasagna noodles
about 2 cups shredded zucchini
¾ pound mozzarella, shredded
1 teaspoon kosher salt

Preheat oven to 350°F. In a medium bowl, lightly beat eggs. Add ricotta cheese, ¼ cup Parmesan, parsley, salt and pepper; stir until well combined. Line the bottom of a 13 x 9-inch baking pan with half of the sliced tomatoes and completely cover tomatoes with half of the basil leaves. Top basil leaves with 3 lasagna noodles. Spread half of the ricotta mixture over lasagna noodles. It won't completely cover the noodles, but don't worry, it spreads out during cooking. Top ricotta mixture with 1·cup of shredded zucchini and top zucchini with half of the mozzarella cheese. Repeat layers, starting with another layer of tomatoes. Top the last layer of mozzarella with remaining ¼ cup of Parmesan; sprinkle top of lasagna with kosher salt and top with chopped tomato. Cover with foil and bake for 45 minutes. Remove foil and let lasagna stand for 15 minutes before serving.

8 to 10 servings

BanzoBurgers

I've veered off the traditional beaten path when it comes to serving these flavorful, hearty and nutritious burgers. No ho-hum hamburger rolls here; we serve these burgers atop crispy yellow tostada shells. While it's a tad messy, the combination of flavors and textures leaves all who eat one looking for seconds.

4 cloves garlic
2 cans (15 ounces each) garbanzo beans, drained
5 tablespoons fresh lemon juice
⅓ cup tahini paste
1 teaspoon salt
½ teaspoon crushed red pepper
¼ cup whole flax seeds, ground
olive oil
6 tostada shells, heated according to package directions
sides of salsa, sour cream, shredded lettuce, alfalfa sprouts, chopped black olives
and chopped avocado

Place garlic in food processor or blender and pulse 4–5 times. Add garbanzo beans, lemon juice, tahini, salt and red pepper. Pulse several times so that mixture is combined but chunky. Transfer to a large bowl, stir in ground flax seeds, and mix until incorporated. Shape into 6 patties. In a large sauté pan, heat about 1 tablespoon olive oil (enough to cover bottom of pan) over moderate heat. Fry burgers for about 1–2 minutes, turn and cook for an additional minute. Place a burger on each tostada shell. Serve immediately and pass the salsa, sour cream, shredded lettuce, alfalfa sprouts, black olives and avocado to your guests.

6 burgers

MEAT, CHICKEN, PORK
Main Dishes

For the sake of your health and for the health of our planet, the most important thing I can share with you about meat is the importance of knowing as much as you can about where it came from, how it was raised and, if you want to take it one step further, how it was harvested. I encourage you to buy certified organic, free-range meat without added growth hormones or antibiotics. (Caution: "authentic" and "natural" are loosely used terms.) Support farmers who use sustainable practices: making use of natural resources without destroying the ecological balance of an area.

While I like meat (people with my blood type are encouraged to eat meat, something I discovered when I became a vegan many years ago and got sick from not eating it), I've cut back because meat has an environmental impact on the planet. Growing meat uses up a lot of resources. It is estimated that livestock production generates nearly a fifth of the world's greenhouse gases— more than what's generated by transportation.

For that reason, this section is one of the smaller sections in *Tasting the Seasons*. Meatloaf is a childhood favorite of mine, and that is the reason there are four recipes devoted to that one basic dish; to me, it's the epitome of comfort food. But in keeping with my attempt to lower meat consumption, I've used meatless ground round, a tofu-based ground beef, in a few of my meatloaf recipes. Taste-testers didn't know the difference.

Country Ham (see page 163) was my grandparents' favorite, and it was served with reverence during the holidays. Sustainable practices weren't an issue back then because sustainable was their natural practice. Hot Bacon and Potato Dinner (see page 156) was a weekly tradition; not only was it delicious, it was inexpensive as well. Other recipes in this section are great for mid-week meals and many are great to serve when entertaining.

So while I am not anti-meat, I like to know where my meat is coming from. The big word is traceability; take full responsibility for knowing the origins of where your meat was sourced.

MEAT, CHICKEN, PORK
Main Dishes

Hot Bacon and Potato Dinner

Chicken Salad with Broccoli and Bacon

Southwest Taco Beef with Cornbread Crust

Global Egg Rolls

Company Chicken

Bourbon Pork with Creamy Mustard Sauce

Tarragon Basil Chicken Salad

Country Ham

MEATLOAF

Classic Meatloaf

Ginger Tomato-Crowned Meatloaf

Apricot-Glazed Meatloaf

Healthy Meatloaf

HOT BACON AND POTATO DINNER

I would be remiss if I didn't pay tribute to my grandparents by featuring this unusual, tasty recipe that has been in my family for generations. The meal was (and still is) fondly known as The Boiled Dinner. It's a wonderfully simple combination of kale, potatoes, hard-boiled eggs and bacon that is customarily chopped and mixed with a knife and fork by each individual diner.

8 eggs
4 medium potatoes, quartered (peeling is a matter of preference)
1 pound dinosaur kale, washed, inner rib removed
12 slices of bacon
1 cup apple cider vinegar
4 tablespoons sugar
salt and pepper, to taste

Fill a medium pot with water and bring to a boil. Add eggs and cook for about 15 minutes. Transfer cooked eggs to a bowl; refill the pot with water and bring to a boil. Add potatoes and cook for about 15 minutes or until fork-tender. Fill a large pot half full with water and bring to a boil. Add kale and cook until tender. When eggs are cool enough to handle, peel off shells. Drain potato water and transfer potatoes to a covered dish to keep warm. Fry bacon until crispy. Pour excess bacon fat from pan. Add apple cider vinegar and sugar to the still-warm bacon pan. Stir until mixture is combined and sugar has dissolved; season with salt and pepper to taste. Keep warm. Evenly distribute kale into four wide, shallow bowls. Top kale with one potato (4 quarters), two eggs and three slices of bacon. Drizzle warm dressing over the mixture. Serve immediately.

4 servings

CHICKEN SALAD WITH BROCCOLI AND BACON

Broccoli and red pepper give this chicken salad its vibrant color, and the crispy bacon adds a marvelous crunch and flavor. Most everything can be prepared in advance, but wait until you're ready to serve before tossing the salad ingredients with the dressing.

¼ cup sour cream
¼ cup mayonnaise
1 tablespoon raspberry vinegar
1 teaspoon dry dill
½ teaspoon dry mustard
¼ teaspoon salt
a few grindings of freshly ground black pepper
2 cups bite-size cooked white meat chicken
2 cups bite-size broccoli florets, cooked until just fork-tender
½ cup chopped red pepper
4 handfuls assorted lettuce leaves
6 slices bacon, cooked until crispy, crumbled

In a small bowl, combine sour cream, mayonnaise and raspberry vinegar. Whisk in dill, mustard, salt and pepper. In a medium bowl, combine chicken, broccoli and red pepper. Toss chicken salad with dressing. Divide lettuce leaves onto 4 serving plates, evenly distribute chicken salad and top each salad with crumbled bacon. Serve immediately.

4 servings

SOUTHWEST TACO BEEF WITH CORNBREAD CRUST

This delicious dish bears some resemblance to the popular Tamale Pie recipe in my first cookbook, *This Book Cooks*. In this rendition I've added colorful carrots, zesty taco seasoning, Kalamata olives and fire-roasted tomatoes. The result is divine.

> 1 teaspoon olive oil
> 2 cloves, garlic, minced
> 1 medium onion, chopped
> 1 medium carrot, shredded
> 1¼ pounds ground beef
> ½ cup water
> 1 package (1.27 ounces) Southwest taco seasoning
> ½ cup pitted and chopped Kalamata olives
> 2 cans (14.5 ounces each) diced fire-roasted tomatoes

Heat olive oil in a large skillet over moderate heat and sauté garlic, chopped onion and shredded carrot until tender. Add ground beef and cook until brown. Drain off any excess fat. Stir in water and taco seasoning and cook for about 5 minutes. Add black olives and fire-roasted tomatoes, and stir until combined. Transfer mixture to a 13 x 9-inch baking dish.

CORNBREAD CRUST
> 1 cup yellow cornmeal
> 2 teaspoons salt
> 1 tablespoon baking powder
> 2 eggs
> 1 cup sour cream
> ⅓ cup olive oil
> 1 can (4 ounces) chopped green chilies
> 1½ cups fresh corn (frozen can be substituted)
> 1 cup shredded cheddar cheese

Preheat oven to 350°F. In a small bowl, combine cornmeal, salt and baking powder. In a large bowl, whisk eggs and add sour cream, olive oil, green chilies, corn and cheddar cheese. Add cornmeal mixture to egg mixture and stir until well combined. Spoon mixture over beef and bake for 45 minutes. Serve immediately.

8 servings

GLOBAL EGG ROLLS

If you can't decide whether to have Chinese, Mexican, Mediterranean or American food, this dish seems to satisfy any of those food cravings. Sides of salsa, sour cream and guacamole are delicious to use for dipping. Marinated Yellow Beets with Horseradish or Kohlrabi Coleslaw (see Index for recipes) both have great texture and are nutritious accompaniments.

1 pound ground beef
½ cup shredded carrots
½ cup sliced green onions
½ cup chickpeas (garbanzo beans)
½ teaspoon salt
a few grindings of freshly ground black pepper
14 egg roll wrappers
1½–2 cups shredded cheddar cheese
canola oil for frying
sides of salsa, sour cream and guacamole

In a sauté pan over moderate heat, cook ground beef until lightly brown. Remove from heat and drain off any excess fat. Add carrots, green onions, chickpeas and salt and pepper. Stir until mixture is evenly distributed. Working with one egg roll wrapper at a time, top the center of wrapper with about 1 tablespoon of cheese and top cheese with about ⅓ cup meat mixture. Fold each side of the wrapper toward the center, roll and moisten exposed edge with water to seal. Place in a single layer on a platter. Repeat process with each wrapper until all the rolls are assembled. Heat oil in a large sauté pan over moderately high heat. Cook egg rolls (in batches of 4–5) until lightly brown. Keep egg rolls in a warm oven until all the rolls are cooked. Serve immediately and pass the sides of salsa, sour cream and guacamole to your guests.

14 rolls

Company Chicken

This recipe is a great choice if you're planning a luncheon.

1 small onion, finely chopped
½ cup finely chopped celery
½ cup finely chopped red pepper
1 cup mayonnaise
½ teaspoon salt
1 teaspoon Worcestershire sauce
freshly ground black pepper
2 pounds white meat chicken, cooked, cut or torn into bite-size pieces
1 cup cubed French or Italian bread
2 tablespoons butter, melted

Preheat oven to 350°F. In a large bowl, combine onion, celery and red pepper with mayonnaise, salt, Worcestershire sauce and black pepper. Add chicken and toss to combine evenly. Transfer to an 8-inch baking dish. Toss bread with melted butter and top chicken with bread cubes. Bake chicken for 25–30 minutes or until heated through. Serve immediately.

6 servings

BOURBON PORK WITH CREAMY MUSTARD SAUCE

I like to serve this dish with the Cranberry Apple Salad with Sunflower Seeds (see Index for recipe), creamy mashed potatoes and steamed green beans.

> ½ *cup low-sodium soy sauce*
> ½ *cup bourbon*
> ½ *cup brown sugar*
> *1 butterflied pork loin (4 pounds)*
> ½ *cup sour cream*
> ½ *cup mayonnaise*
> *1 tablespoon Dijon-style mustard*
> *1 teaspoon apple cider vinegar*
> *1 tablespoon dry mustard*
> ½ *teaspoon salt*
> *2 tablespoons minced green onion*

In a container that will accommodate the pork loin, combine soy sauce, bourbon and brown sugar. Stir until sugar is nearly dissolved. Place pork in dish and turn to evenly coat on both sides. Marinate in the refrigerator for 3–4 hours. In a medium bowl, combine sour cream, mayonnaise, mustard and vinegar and mix until well blended. Stir in dry mustard, salt and green onions. Refrigerate until serving time. Preheat oven to 350°F. Roll the pork loin and bind crosswise at 2-inch intervals with butcher's twine or kitchen string. Transfer to a baking dish and top with bourbon marinade. Bake pork for about 45 minutes, basting with marinade once during cooking. Let stand about 15 minutes before cutting twine or string. Carve the pork into thin slices. Pass the creamy mustard sauce to your guests.

8 servings

Tarragon Basil Chicken Salad

Here's a unique variation on the traditional chicken salad recipe. Chicken breasts are slathered with Dijon-style mustard, and seasoned with tarragon and basil and then baked. It's a marvelous combination of flavors.

1½ pounds chicken breasts, skinned and boned
¼ cup Dijon-style mustard
1 tablespoon dried tarragon
1 tablespoon dried basil
1 cup minced celery
⅓ cup mayonnaise (more or less to taste)
salt to taste (optional)

Preheat oven to 350°F. Arrange chicken in a single layer in a baking dish. Spread mustard evenly over chicken, and top with tarragon and basil. Bake for 45 minutes. Allow chicken to cool before cutting into bite-size pieces. In a large bowl, combine chicken, celery and mayonnaise; season with salt to taste. Toss to evenly distribute ingredients. Refrigerate until ready to serve.

4 servings

COUNTRY HAM

Country ham was served at most holiday dinners throughout my childhood, and my best memories have always been the salty flavor of the ham and the wonderful aroma that wafted from the kitchen. A true holiday classic! After the ham has cooked it needs to be refrigerated overnight before slicing paper-thin. This ham recipe produces a large yield, making it a great choice if you're hosting a big group. Country Ham, aka Smithfield, Virginia and Kentucky Country Ham, can generally be found in independently owned meat stores and small grocery stores. Remember to reserve the ham essence for bean soup stock.

one country ham

Have the butcher remove about 4–5 inches of the ham hock. Remove the rind, pepper and most of the fat from the ham. Place ham on a rack in a large stovetop pan; the broiler pan that comes with most stoves works well. Add about 1–2 inches of water. Cover ham tightly, bring to a boil then lower heat to simmer. Cook for about 2–3 hours, turning the ham mid-way through cooking time. Add more water to pan if necessary.

Allow the ham to cool for several hours before refrigerating overnight.

Serves a crowd

CLASSIC MEATLOAF

Meatloaf was one of my favorite meals when I was growing up. My mother prepared a traditional recipe. Ground beef was mixed with eggs, cracker crumbs and dried onion soup mix and topped with tomato sauce or ketchup. I've taken her traditional meatloaf recipe and added some zing to it. It always was, and still is, a true crowd pleaser.

2 eggs
½ cup quick cooking oatmeal, uncooked
1 package onion dip mix
2 pounds ground beef
1 can (8 ounces) tomato sauce
2 tablespoons brown sugar
2 tablespoons apple cider vinegar
1 tablespoon Worcestershire sauce
1 teaspoon Dijon-style mustard

Preheat oven to 350°F. In a large bowl, whisk eggs, and add oatmeal, onion soup mix and ground beef and mix until egg mixture is fully combined with meat. Shape into a rectangle and place in an 11 x 7-inch baking dish. In a medium bowl, combine tomato sauce, brown sugar, vinegar, Worcestershire sauce and mustard. Pour over meatloaf. Bake uncovered for 1 hour. Serve immediately.

8 servings

GINGER TOMATO-CROWNED MEATLOAF

I love the aroma that wafts through the house when any meatloaf is cooking in the oven, just as I love how appreciative family and friends are when you've prepared a home-cooked, comfort food meal for them. This meatloaf is sure to satisfy on both levels. It puts an unusual twist on the tried-and-true ketchup or tomato sauce topping. A ginger glaze covers this loaf, with delicious results. The addition of shredded raw carrots and zucchini add beneficial nutrients and color and also keep the meatloaf moist. Serve with mashed potatoes and peas for comfort food heaven.

2 pounds lean ground beef
1 cup shredded carrots
1 cup shredded zucchini
¾ cup minced fresh parsley
¾ cup chopped onion
2 eggs
1 tablespoon Worcestershire sauce
1 teaspoon Dijon-style mustard
1 teaspoon salt
freshly ground black pepper
1 cup ketchup
¼ cup brown sugar
2 teaspoons ground ginger

Preheat oven to 375°F. In a large bowl, combine ground beef with carrots, zucchini, parsley and onion. In a small bowl, combine eggs, Worcestershire sauce, mustard, salt and pepper. Whisk until well combined. Add to meat mixture and mix until ingredients are evenly distributed. Transfer to a 13 x 9-inch baking dish and shape mixture into a rectangular or oval loaf. In a small bowl, combine ketchup, brown sugar and ground ginger; mix until well blended. Spoon ginger tomato glaze mixture over meatloaf and bake uncovered for 45 minutes. Serve immediately.

8 servings

Apricot-Glazed Meatloaf

I've always been a big fan of meatloaf. It's perhaps the first grown-up comfort food that many of us were introduced to as children. My Apricot-Glazed Meatloaf takes the traditional meatloaf recipe to another level by adding nutritional ingredients that enhance and enrich as well as add color and boost flavor. In this recipe, as with Healthy Meatloaf (see page 167), I've folded meatless ground round into the loaf along with the lean ground beef.

1 teaspoon olive oil
½ cup finely chopped onion
½ cup finely chopped celery
½ cup finely chopped red pepper
1 cup finely chopped white mushrooms (about 4 medium)
½ cup shredded carrot
½ cup pitted and chopped Kalamata black olives
1 tablespoon prepared horseradish
1 teaspoon dry mustard
1 teaspoon salt
several grindings of freshly ground black pepper
1¼ pounds lean ground beef
1 package (12 ounces) meatless ground round
½ cup apricot preserves
½ cup tomato sauce
1 tablespoon Worcestershire sauce

Preheat oven to 350°F. Heat olive oil in a medium sauté pan over moderate heat. Sauté onion, celery, red pepper and mushrooms for about 3–5 minutes or until just tender. In a large bowl, combine carrot, olives, horseradish, dry mustard, salt and black pepper. Add sautéed vegetables, ground beef and meatless ground round and mix until ingredients are well distributed. Transfer meat mixture to a 13 x 9-inch pan and shape into a rectangular loaf. In a small bowl, whisk apricot preserves, tomato sauce and Worcestershire sauce until combined. Spoon the apricot glaze mixture over the meatloaf and bake, uncovered for 1 hour. Serve immediately.

8 servings

HEALTHY MEATLOAF

In my quest for healthy replacement ingredients, I discovered that combining ground beef with a meatless ground round makes for an airy, light-textured meatloaf. If you happen to have any leftovers, you're in for a remarkable meatloaf sandwich, hot or cold. Nick's Potato Salad (see Index for recipe) and wilted spinach are wonderful accompaniments to this dish.

1 teaspoon olive oil
½ cup chopped red pepper
½ cup chopped celery
1 medium onion, chopped
¼ cup freshly grated Parmesan cheese
½ cup shredded raw carrot
1 tablespoon prepared horseradish
1 teaspoon Dijon-style mustard
½ teaspoon salt
freshly ground black pepper
1¼ pounds lean ground beef
1 package (12 ounces) meatless ground round
½ cup ketchup

Preheat oven to 350°F. Heat olive oil in a medium sauté pan over moderate heat and sauté red pepper, celery and onion for about 3–5 minutes or until tender. Remove from heat. In a large bowl, combine Parmesan cheese, shredded carrot, horseradish, mustard, salt and pepper. Add ground beef and meatless ground round and mix until ingredients are evenly distributed. Once sautéed vegetables have cooled slightly, add to meat mixture and combine well. Place in an 11 x 7-inch baking dish and form into an oval shape. Spread ketchup evenly over meatloaf and bake for 45 minutes. Serve immediately.

6 servings

COLD GARDEN GREENERY
Side Dishes

Side dishes are a great complement to almost any meal. They typically add color, balance, variety and added nutrients: all helpful attributes when planning a menu. Color is important; if your meal is visually attractive, eaters are more likely to appreciate and indulge. Balance and variety are vital for optimum nutrition. Eating foods at the height of their growing seasons, when food is at its peak flavor, affords you the most nutrients.

Whenever my mother made lettuce-leaf salads for us when we were growing up, she always put them together from whatever ingredients she had on hand. As children, we grew to love her salad combinations. Our salads were never tossed with store-bought dressing, and because I grew up seeing how quickly my mother whipped up something fabulous from scratch, I'm constantly amazed when people tell me it takes too long to prepare homemade dressing. It takes me longer to read and decipher the list of ingredients on a bottle of commercial salad dressing than the minimal time it takes to combine a few fresh ingredients to make a delicious, healthy dressing. See Enhancers: Salad Dressings, pages 29-33.

Tips for preparing lettuce-leaf salads

• Cherry tomatoes, julienned carrots, sliced mushrooms, shredded radicchio, bell peppers, sprouts, onions, avocado, black olives, apples, grapes, pears, oranges, grapefruit and dried cranberries are just some of the wonderful salad toppers that can be added to greens.

• Toasted nuts and croutons add a welcome crunch to any salad.

• Those convenient, pre-packaged, "triple-washed," "ready to eat" greens (typically in un-eco-friendly plastic boxes or bags) have been found to contain bacteria. These lettuce leaves are sometimes washed in a diluted chlorine solution or fumigated with ozone, a type of processing known as "value-added." It's best to purchase heads of lettuce.

• If you're plating individual salads for a sit-down dinner party, allow one heavy handful of lettuce leaves per person. For a large gathering and buffet style service, allow 1½ handfuls per person.

• Salad dressing should be served at room temperature.

- It is best to toss lettuce-leaf salads just prior to serving.

- Dressing should just "coat" the leaves; too much dressing will result in a soggy salad.

- Toss lettuce and weighted ingredients separately.

- Weighted toppings (tomatoes, carrots, peas, nuts, eggs, dried fruit, etc.) tend to sink, so pre-plate salad greens for small gatherings and then top each salad with the heavier ingredients.

- For larger gatherings or buffet style set ups, serve salad from a rimmed platter or a shallow bowl rather than a deep bowl to avoid having the heavy ingredients sink.

- Lettuce-leaf salads are generally not good keepers and rarely make good leftovers.

I hope you enjoy all of the recipes in this section. You're going to find simple lettuce-leaf salads, as well as heartier combinations that are "family friendly" salads, to serve with a casual supper or at an elegant dinner party.

COLD GARDEN GREENERY
Side Dishes

Traditional Spinach Salad

Leafy Greens with Radish and Eggs

Honeyed Pecan Salad with Tangerine Vinaigrette

Cranberry Apple Salad with Sunflower Seeds

Arugula Salad with Halloumi

Apple Celery Salad with Peanut Vinaigrette

Curried Red, White and Green Vegetables

Fruity, Nutty, Blue-Cheesy Spinach Salad

Kohlrabi Coleslaw

Herb-Dressed Cabbage Salad

Marinated Yellow Beets with Horseradish

Rainbow Radish Rice

Marinated Potatoes

TRADITIONAL SPINACH SALAD

Choose mushrooms that are white and firm. The amount of bacon you use is a matter of preference; about 1½ slices per salad seems to be just right.

Prepare **Apple Cider Celery Seed Dressing** (see page 33)

> *8 generous handfuls baby spinach*
> *8 medium mushrooms, sliced*
> *8 hard-boiled eggs, chopped*
> *8–12 slices bacon, cooked until crisp*
> *8 slices red onion, thinly sliced*

In a large bowl, toss spinach with Apple Cider Celery Seed Dressing until lightly coated. Divide spinach evenly among 8 salad plates or shallow bowls. Top each salad with mushroom slices, chopped egg, bacon and red onion. Serve immediately.

8 servings

Leafy Greens with Radish and Eggs

I love any salad that has toasted sunflower seeds and hard-boiled eggs as ingredients. The seeds give a salad an extra crunchiness, and chopped egg lends an additional depth of texture; plus the yolk blends with the dressing for added creaminess. With this recipe, I've focused on those two ingredients and added sliced radish for extra crunch and a pop of color.

Prepare **Tarragon Dressing** (see page 31)

> *8 generous handfuls of assorted lettuce leaves, torn*
> *8 hard-boiled eggs, sliced*
> *8 radishes, thinly sliced*
> *½ cup sunflower seeds, toasted and salted*

In a large bowl, toss salad greens with just enough Tarragon Dressing to lightly coat the leaves. Divide greens among 8 serving plates and top each salad with egg slices, radish slices and sunflower seeds. Serve immediately.

8 servings

Honeyed Pecan Salad with Tangerine Vinaigrette

Radicchio is an exotic Italian salad ingredient related to chicory. Its garnet color adds vibrancy to tossed green salads. Radicchio has a peppery flavor that is countered in this salad by the sweetened nuts and Tangerine Vinaigrette.

Tangerine Vinaigrette

1 tablespoon sugar
1 teaspoon dry mustard
1 teaspoon salt
2 tablespoons seasoned rice vinegar
½ cup tangerine juice
½ cup canola oil

In a 2-cup jar with a tight-fitting lid, combine sugar, dry mustard and salt. Add rice vinegar, tangerine juice and canola oil.

1 cup pecan halves
⅛ cup honey
1 teaspoon sugar
8 handfuls Boston lettuce leaves, torn into bite-size pieces
1 cup shredded radicchio
1 tangerine, peeled, sectioned and cut in half width-wise
¼ cup dried cranberries

Preheat oven to 325°F. On a parchment-lined, rimmed baking sheet, toss pecans with honey; arrange in a single layer and bake for 12–15 minutes. Transfer nuts to a piece of foil that has been lightly coated with cooking spray. Sprinkle nuts with sugar; set aside. In a large bowl, toss Boston lettuce leaves with radicchio. Shake vinaigrette and lightly coat lettuce leaves with dressing (you will have extra vinaigrette: refrigerate unused portion). Divide lettuce onto 8 salad plates. Top lettuce leaves with tangerine pieces, cranberries and honeyed pecans. Serve immediately.

8 servings

CRANBERRY APPLE SALAD WITH SUNFLOWER SEEDS

When I served this salad at a family birthday dinner, it got rave reviews, even from my brother's three kids. This is the perfect salad to prepare during the fall and winter months; it complements hearty meats, soups, stews and casseroles that are typically served this time of year. Bourbon Pork with Creamy Mustard Sauce (see page 161) goes wonderfully with this salad. Once apples are cut and exposed to the air, they turn brown fairly quickly; chop the apple just prior to serving.

Prepare **Apple Cider Celery Seed Dressing** (see page 33)

5 cups white cabbage, shredded
1½ cups sliced celery, ¼-inch size pieces
1 large apple, chopped
⅓ cup dried cranberries
⅓ cup toasted sunflower seeds

In a large bowl, combine cabbage, celery, chopped apple, cranberries and sunflower seeds. Toss the salad with the Apple Cider Celery Seed Dressing with just enough dressing to coat the ingredients. Serve immediately.

8 servings

ARUGULA SALAD WITH HALLOUMI

The first time I ate rocket, we were vacationing in St. Lucia. When the waiter presented me with the Rocket Salad Special, I was quite surprised to see what appeared to be arugula on my plate. I later learned that on the island, arugula is called rocket. So much for stumbling upon a new food! However, in my rendition of that wonderful salad, I've paired rocket/arugula with one of my all-time favorite food discoveries, halloumi cheese. Halloumi is salty, so if you're watching your salt intake, omit this ingredient from the vinaigrette recipe. Halloumi can be found in the specialty foods refrigerated section of most grocery stores.

1 teaspoon salt
several grindings of freshly ground black pepper
1 teaspoon Dijon-style mustard
¼ cup apple cider vinegar
¾ cup olive oil
8 generous handfuls of arugula
canola oil for frying
1 package (8.8 ounce) halloumi cheese, cut into eight ¼-inch slices

In a 2-cup jar with a tight-fitting lid, combine salt, pepper, mustard, apple cider vinegar and olive oil. Cover and shake until ingredients are combined. Keep vinaigrette at room temperature until ready to use. Shake vinaigrette and toss with greens, just enough to coat the leaves. Divide greens among 8 salad plates. Cover the bottom of a large sauté pan with oil, and over moderate heat, sauté halloumi cheese until light golden brown (browning will be uneven), about 1–2 minutes per side. Top each salad with a slice of cheese. Serve immediately.

8 servings

APPLE CELERY SALAD WITH PEANUT VINAIGRETTE

Once apples are cut and exposed to the air they turn brown, but you can prepare the remaining salad ingredients, as well as the dressing, ahead of time. Leftover dressing will keep for several days in the refrigerator.

¼ cup seasoned rice vinegar
½ teaspoon salt
3 teaspoons sugar
a few drops Tabasco sauce or hot pepper sauce
1 cup canola oil
½ cup chunky natural peanut butter
4 cups finely shredded white cabbage
2 cups sliced celery
2 cups chopped Gala apple (or any crisp variety)

In a medium bowl, combine vinegar, salt, sugar and Tabasco or hot pepper sauce. Slowly whisk in canola oil and continue to whisk until well blended. Add peanut butter and whisk until ingredients are incorporated. In a medium bowl, toss cabbage with celery. Add chopped apple to cabbage/celery mixture. Toss with just enough dressing to coat the ingredients. Serve immediately.

8 servings

CURRIED RED, WHITE AND GREEN VEGETABLES

This is a cheery-colored, wonderfully textured side dish that will disappear quickly.

½ cup mayonnaise
1½ teaspoons sugar
1 tablespoon apple cider vinegar
1 teaspoon curry powder
¼ teaspoon salt
3 cups cauliflower florets broken into bite-size pieces
½ cup sliced sweet onion
½ cup chopped red pepper
½ cup frozen peas, thawed
½ cup shredded sharp cheddar cheese

In a small bowl, combine mayonnaise, sugar, apple cider vinegar, curry powder and salt. Mix until well blended. Cover and refrigerate overnight or for at about 3–4 hours. Steam the cauliflower until just fork-tender. Let cauliflower cool to room temperature. In a medium bowl, combine cauliflower, onion, red pepper, peas and grated cheddar cheese. Toss with dressing and serve immediately.

6 servings

FRUITY, NUTTY, BLUE-CHEESY SPINACH SALAD

Choose pears that are ripe and slightly fragrant but still firm. Once pears are cut and exposed to the air, they turn brown; best to do your pear preparing just prior to serving. If pears aren't in season, replace them with mandarin orange segments.

Prepare **Fresh-Squeezed Orange Dressing** (see page 32)

> *8 generous handfuls fresh baby spinach*
> *2 pears (peeling is a matter of preference), cut into bite-size pieces*
> *½ cup chopped walnuts, toasted*
> *½ cup dried cranberries*
> *½ cup crumbled blue cheese*

In a large bowl, toss spinach with Fresh-Squeezed Orange Dressing, just enough to coat the leaves. Divide spinach equally among 8 serving plates. Top each salad with pears, walnuts, cranberries and crumbled blue cheese, distributing ingredients evenly. Serve immediately.

8 servings

KOHLRABI COLESLAW

I was first introduced to kohlrabi by Joan Norman, co-owner of One Straw Farm, Maryland's largest organic vegetable farm. She and her husband Drew "had a garden and a dream" more than 25 years ago, and they're still going strong. Needless to say, I couldn't wait to get home and begin testing recipes with this unusual new find. After trying several methods of preparation, I focused on shredding this cabbage/turnip veggie into a salad. Think coleslaw. This dish has been lauded for its texture and mellow flavor. It's been described as "sweeter and milder than traditional cabbage slaw," and it's a perfect accompaniment to barbecued meats and sandwiches. This slaw can be prepared in advance, but wait until just before serving to cut up the avocado and toss in the sunflower seeds.

> ½ cup mayonnaise
> 1 teaspoon sugar
> ½ teaspoon salt
> freshly ground black pepper, to taste
> 6 small kohlrabies, peeled and shredded
> 1 ripe avocado, cut into bite-size pieces
> ¼ cup toasted sunflower seeds

In a medium bowl, combine mayonnaise with sugar, salt and pepper to taste. Add shredded kohlrabi and mix well. Add avocado and sunflower seeds to kohlrabi mixture and toss to combine. Serve immediately.

6 servings

HERB-DRESSED CABBAGE SALAD

The multi-herb and olive oil mixture delivers an intense pop to the sometimes boring, often unappreciated cabbage salad.

> *½ cup olive oil*
> *1 teaspoon salt*
> *1 teaspoon oregano*
> *1 teaspoon dried minced onion*
> *1 teaspoon basil*
> *1 teaspoon marjoram*
> *1 teaspoon thyme*
> *6 cups thinly sliced white cabbage*

In a 1-cup jar with a tight-fitting lid, combine olive oil, salt, oregano, granulated onion, basil, marjoram and thyme. Shake vigorously. In a large bowl, toss cabbage with herb and olive oil mixture. Serve immediately.

6 servings

Marinated Yellow Beets with Horseradish

If you're a fan of beets, you will find this colorful side dish to be as tasty as it is beautiful. The blend of flavors is at its peak when served at room temperature. If yellow beets aren't available, use the more common red ones.

> *1 bunch yellow beets (about 3–4 medium), quartered*
> *2 tablespoons olive oil*
> *2 tablespoons horseradish*
> *2 tablespoons seasoned rice vinegar*
> *½ teaspoon salt*

In a large pot, boil beets until fork-tender. When beets are cool enough to handle, gently remove skin. Julienne-cut the beets and place them in a serving bowl. In a small bowl, combine olive oil, horseradish, vinegar and salt. Add to the beets and toss until evenly coated. Cover and let marinate at room temperature for 30 minutes or longer.

6 servings

RAINBOW RADISH RICE

A colorful and complementary combination of ingredients that's as delicious with barbecued chicken wings as it is with Poached Cod on Lemon Beds (see page 133).

Prepare **Kerry's All Purpose Vinaigrette** (see page 29)

> *3 cups white rice, cooked, room temperature*
> *1¼ cups frozen peas, thawed*
> *1 cup halved and thinly sliced radishes*
> *1 cup halved yellow cherry tomatoes*
> *½ cup thinly sliced celery*
> *½ cup sliced green onions*
> *½ cup sliced orange pepper*
> *½ cup black Kalamata olives, pitted*
> *1 tablespoon minced fresh parsley*
> *freshly ground black pepper, to taste*

In a large bowl, combine rice, peas, radishes, cherry tomatoes, celery, onions, pepper, olives, parsley and pepper to taste. Toss with just enough dressing to lightly coat the ingredients. Serve immediately.

6 to 8 servings

Marinated Potatoes

My mother has been serving this potato dish since she and my father first ate it at a picnic with friends in the summer of 1945. The picnic was in honor of their return from the war. It was a potluck event, and one of the women brought this potato dish, announcing it wasn't at all like traditional potato salad because it only had a tablespoon of mayonnaise. (Mayonnaise was being rationed at the time.) Everyone loved it and no one missed the traditional potato salad laden with mayonnaise.

> ½ cup canola oil
> ¼ cup seasoned rice vinegar
> 1 teaspoon celery seed
> 1 teaspoon salt
> ¾ teaspoon black pepper
> 6 medium potatoes, unpeeled (peel if you prefer), quartered
> 1½ cups quartered and thinly sliced onion
> 1 tablespoon mayonnaise

In a 1-cup jar with a tight-fitting lid, combine oil, vinegar, celery seed, salt and pepper. Shake contents until well combined. Allow marinade to stand at room temperature for several hours. Cook potatoes in boiling, salted water for about 15 minutes or until tender. Allow the potatoes to cool. When cool enough to handle, thinly slice. In the dish you will be serving the potato salad, layer the potatoes and the onions alternately. Shake marinade and pour evenly over the potatoes and onions. Cover and refrigerate for several hours or overnight. Just before serving, toss the potatoes with the mayonnaise. Season with additional salt if necessary.

6 servings

Introducing

WARM GARDEN GREENERY
Side Dishes

My mother was so clever when she prepared vegetables for our family; she made them taste so great we couldn't resist eating them. She did what every parent should do: for optimum taste results, she bought vegetables at the height of their growing seasons. She prepared them with interesting, natural and healthy seasonings, and she always accompanied vegetable side dishes with complementing main entrees, with much thought given to color, balance, variety and nutrition.

So if you're a parent, and want your kids to grow up eating their vegetables, do what my mother did. To this day, her brood of five chooses vegetables over any other food.

WARM GARDEN GREENERY
Side Dishes

Baked Garlic

Creamy Carrots

Spinach Gratin

Cheesy Shredded Potatoes

Creamy Potatoes Au Gratin

A Maize Zing Corn Pudding

Roasted Romano Red Potatoes

Purple Cabbage Pure and Simple

Parsley Parmesan Garlic Stuffing

Sweet Potato Leaves with Sweet Dressing

Lemon Butter Brussels Sprouts, Sauerkraut-Style

Caramelized Parsnips with Roasted Pecans

Mushroom and Robiola Cheese Polenta Pie

Buttery Mushroom Bread Pudding

Pumpernickel Parmesan Polenta

Caramelized Carrots with Kalamata Olives

Nick's Potato Salad

Basic Bread Stuffing

Carrot and Leek Gratin

Berry Nutty Couscous

Globe Artichokes

Chinese Broccoli

Sauerkraut

BAKED GARLIC

When garlic is baked whole, it has a milder, sweeter flavor than raw garlic, making it a delicious accompaniment to beef, especially steak. If you're a garlic fan, Baked Garlic is addictive; Nick and I can each eat a whole head.

4 heads garlic, cut in half widthwise
olive oil
coarse sea salt

Preheat oven to 400°F. Place garlic halves on a rimmed baking sheet, exposed garlic side up. Drizzle olive oil over garlic and sprinkle with salt. Bake for about 10 minutes. Turn halves over so the garlic side is facing down and bake an additional 10 minutes or until fork-tender and lightly browned. Watch closely once garlic begins to brown; it darkens quickly. Serve immediately.

4 servings

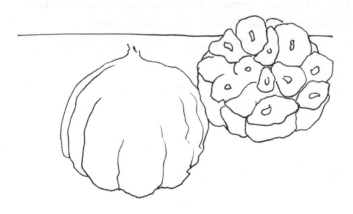

CREAMY CARROTS

If you're a carrot lover, this one is for you.

10 medium carrots, peeled, sliced and cooked until tender
2 tablespoons butter
2 tablespoons minced onion
½ cup minced green pepper
1 tablespoon unbleached all-purpose flour
1 tablespoon sugar
1 cup milk
1 teaspoon salt
freshly ground black pepper, to taste

Preheat oven to 350°F. In a food processor or blender, purée carrots (in batches if necessary) until smooth, then transfer to a large mixing bowl. In a sauté pan over medium heat, melt butter and cook onion and green pepper until golden brown. Whisk in flour and sugar; gradually add milk, stirring constantly until mixture thickens. Combine with puréed carrots and blend well. Add salt and season with pepper to taste. Spoon mixture into a lightly oiled 2-quart casserole dish and bake for 30 minutes or until heated through. Serve immediately.

6 servings

SPINACH GRATIN

This is a wonderful complement to seafood, beef and chicken.

2 tablespoons butter
2 cups sliced white onion
16 ounces frozen chopped spinach, defrosted, drained, and squeezed dry
1 cup heavy cream
1 cup milk
2 eggs
3 tablespoons horseradish
1 teaspoon salt
freshly ground black pepper, to taste
½ cup shredded cheddar cheese
¼ cup dry bread crumbs

Preheat oven to 350°F. In a medium skillet over moderate heat, melt butter; add sliced onion and sauté until translucent. Remove from heat, stir in spinach and combine until evenly distributed. Spoon spinach/onion mixture into a lightly oiled 2-quart baking dish. In a medium bowl, using a wire whisk, combine cream, milk, eggs, horseradish, salt and pepper to taste. Pour over spinach/onion mixture. Bake uncovered for 30 minutes. In a small bowl, combine cheddar cheese and bread crumbs. Blend well and sprinkle over spinach/onion mixture. Bake an additional 25 minutes. Serve immediately.

6 servings

CHEESY SHREDDED POTATOES

These crowd-pleasing potatoes complement chicken, pork and beef.

> *2 teaspoons salt*
> *8–10 medium potatoes (about 3–3½ pounds), unpeeled, quartered*
> *16 ounces sour cream*
> *1 cup shredded cheddar cheese*
> *½ cup (1 stick) butter, melted*
> *¼ cup thinly sliced green onions*
> *1½ teaspoons salt*
> *several grindings of freshly ground black pepper*

Cook the potatoes in salted, boiling water until just fork-tender. Drain potatoes and allow them to cool before refrigerating overnight.

Preheat oven to 350°F. Remove potatoes skins and shred potatoes. Transfer to a large bowl. In a medium bowl, combine sour cream with shredded cheddar cheese. Stir in melted butter, green onions, salt and pepper. Add sour cream mixture to potatoes and gently combine until ingredients are well incorporated. Transfer potatoes to a lightly oiled 4-quart casserole dish. Cover and bake for about 40 minutes or until heated through. Serve immediately.

12 servings

CREAMY POTATOES AU GRATIN

My mother often used what she called "potato water" (the water in which potatoes were boiled) as a base for soups and casseroles. The addition of potato water in this recipe makes these potatoes creamier than most au gratin dishes.

6–8 medium potatoes, cooked and sliced
3 tablespoons butter
3 tablespoons unbleached all-purpose flour
1½ cups potato water
1 cup heavy cream
1 teaspoon dried thyme
1 teaspoon garlic powder
1 teaspoon salt
several grindings of freshly ground black pepper
1½ cups shredded Edam cheese
1 cup cubed slightly stale French bread with crust

Preheat oven to 400°F. Arrange sliced potatoes in a lightly oiled 3-quart baking dish. In a large saucepan over moderate heat, melt butter and whisk in flour 1 tablespoon at a time. Slowly whisk in potato water until mixture is smooth. Lower heat and stir in cream, thyme, garlic powder, salt and pepper. Stir in cheese. When cheese has melted and is fully incorporated, pour over potatoes. Top the potatoes with bread cubes and bake for 20 minutes or until bubbly. Switch oven to broil and broil until bread cubes are golden brown. Serve immediately.

8 servings

A Maize Zing Corn Pudding

This dish is so popular, guests invariably return for seconds and sometimes thirds. I recommend doubling the recipe if you're entertaining hearty eaters.

4 eggs
2 tablespoons unbleached all-purpose flour
6 tablespoons sugar
1½ teaspoons salt
1½ cups milk
4 cups fresh cooked corn
6 tablespoons butter, cut into chunks

Preheat oven to 350°F. In a medium bowl, whisk eggs. Add flour and whisk until well incorporated. Add sugar, salt and milk; stir in corn and pour into a generously oiled 2-liter casserole dish. Dot the top of the corn mixture with chunks of butter. Bake uncovered for 45 minutes, then set oven to broil and brown the top. Serve immediately.

8 servings

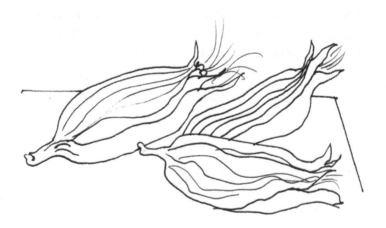

ROASTED ROMANO RED POTATOES

Romano cheese is one of the world's oldest cheeses. This traditional Italian cheese, named after the city of Rome, is a sheep's milk cheese that is slightly sharper, saltier and dryer than Parmesan. There are different types of Romano cheese; my Romano of choice is Pecorino. Roasted Romano Red Potatoes are incredibly simple to prepare, yet they make an elegant accompaniment to meat, chicken and fish.

4 tablespoons olive oil
8 medium red potatoes, unpeeled and quartered
1 cup fresh grated Pecorino Romano cheese

Preheat oven to 400°F. Pour olive oil in a small, shallow bowl. Dip each of the two cut sides of the quartered potatoes in olive oil, then dip the same two sides in Romano cheese. Place potatoes on a parchment-lined, rimmed baking sheet and bake for 35–40 minutes or until fork-tender and lightly browned. Serve immediately.

8 servings

PURPLE CABBAGE PURE AND SIMPLE

This dish is simple to prepare and incredibly versatile—a delicious complement to fish, pork and chicken.

> *½ cup (1 stick) butter*
> *12 cups shredded purple cabbage*
> *1 teaspoon salt*

In a large pot over moderate heat, melt butter. Add cabbage and stir to evenly coat with butter. Cover, reduce heat to low and cook cabbage until tender, about 15 minutes. Add salt and stir to fully combine. Serve immediately.

8 to 10 servings

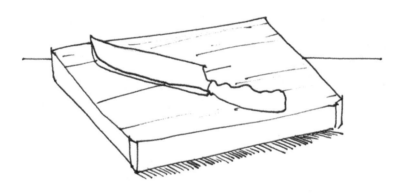

PARSLEY PARMESAN GARLIC STUFFING

This unique combination of ingredients translates into an equally unique stuffing that works as well with baked or grilled fish as it does with baked or grilled chicken.

4 cups cubed bread
1 cup chicken broth
⅛ cup olive oil
½ cup chopped fresh parsley
⅓ cup fresh grated Parmesan cheese
⅛ cup minced garlic

Preheat oven to 350F°. In a medium bowl, toss bread cubes with chicken broth and olive oil. Add parsley, Parmesan cheese and garlic. Toss until ingredients are well distributed. Lightly oil a 1-quart baking dish. Transfer stuffing into dish, cover and bake for 30–40 minutes. Serve immediately.

4 servings

SWEET POTATO LEAVES WITH SWEET DRESSING

The sweet potato leaf is the vine from which sweet potatoes grow. The heart-shaped leaves are similar in color, texture and taste to spinach. When cooked, sweet potato leaves wilt and shrink much like spinach, but the leaf is heartier and not as watery. Sunflower seeds give this dish a surprise crunch, but for variations, the same amount of sautéed garlic or prepared horseradish can be used in place of the nuts, with quite tasty results.

2 bunches sweet potato leaves, stems removed, roughly chopped
2 tablespoons olive oil
2 tablespoons raw sunflower seeds
3 tablespoons seasoned rice vinegar
1 teaspoon sugar
salt and pepper

In a large pot, steam sweet potato leaves until fork-tender, about 5 minutes. Transfer steamed sweet potato leaves to a shallow serving bowl. Cover and keep warm. Heat olive oil in a medium skillet over moderate heat. Add sunflower seeds and sauté, stirring often, for about 1–2 minutes; watch closely so the seeds don't burn. Remove from heat. Add seasoned rice vinegar (stand back as the vinegar will splatter) and sugar. Stir until well blended. Add the vinegar mixture to the sweet potato leaves and toss to combine. Season the dish with salt and pepper. Serve immediately.

4 servings

LEMON BUTTER BRUSSELS SPROUTS, SAUERKRAUT-STYLE

The first memory I have of Brussels sprouts appearing on a dinner plate was when I was in my late teens. My mother introduced them around Thanksgiving time and served them alongside stuffed pork chops and sweet potatoes. Not only was the combination seasonal and colorful, the Brussels sprouts were cooked and seasoned to perfection. Many years later, I thought about how clever my mother was to wait until her brood of five was mature enough to fully appreciate this sophisticated little vegetable.

1½ pounds Brussels sprouts (about 2 dozen)
½ cup (1 stick) butter
1 teaspoon salt
2 tablespoons lemon zest
2 tablespoons lemon juice
a few grindings of freshly ground black pepper

To prepare Brussels sprouts, remove stem, cut in half lengthwise and thinly slice each half widthwise. In a large pan, melt butter over moderate heat, add Brussels sprouts and salt and stir to evenly coat shredded sprouts with butter. Cover, reduce heat to medium-low and cook for 10–15 minutes, stirring occasionally. Add lemon zest and juice, stir, cover and cook an additional 2–5 minutes or until tender. Season the Brussels sprouts with pepper. Serve immediately.

8 servings

CARAMELIZED PARSNIPS WITH ROASTED PECANS

The wonderful sweetness of the parsnips comes out when caramelized. This simple side dish is a great accompaniment to baked chicken.

3–4 tablespoons canola oil
1 pound parsnips, peeled and sliced about ¼-inch thick
4–6 cloves garlic, sliced
¼ cup roughly chopped pecans, toasted and salted

Heat 2 tablespoons of oil in a large skillet over moderate heat. Add and sauté parsnips for about 10–15 minutes, stirring often. Add additional 1–2 tablespoons oil and sliced garlic and cook for another 10 minutes, stirring frequently. Cook until parsnips are slightly blackened and cooked through. Toss with pecans and serve immediately.

4 servings

MUSHROOM AND ROBIOLA CHEESE POLENTA PIE

Robiola cheese is a soft, moist and very flavorful Brie-like melting cheese that gives this dish its decadent flavor and creamy texture. Originating in northern Italy, robiola is starting to rival gorgonzola as that country's most famous cheese. This pie is versatile; pair it with chicken, fish or beef and serve it at breakfast, brunch, lunch or dinner. If you happen to have any leftovers, wedges of pie are delicious when topped with a poached egg. Stand back when adding the cornmeal to the boiling broth because the mixture will splatter. Robiola cheese can be found in specialty cheese shops or Whole Foods Market.

4 cups chicken broth
1 teaspoon salt
1 cup yellow cornmeal
2 tablespoons butter
1 pound white mushrooms, chopped
2 tablespoons cooking sherry
½ teaspoon salt
a few grindings of freshly ground black pepper
¼ pound robiola cheese, cubed

Heat chicken broth in a large deep pot over moderately high heat and bring to a gentle boil. Stir in salt. Reduce heat slightly and slowly add cornmeal, whisking constantly. Reduce heat to low and cook, whisking often, for 15–20 minutes or until thickened. Remove from heat, and transfer cornmeal mixture into a lightly oiled pie plate. Spread the mixture evenly over the bottom of the pie plate.

Preheat oven to 350°F. In a large skillet, melt butter over medium heat, add mushrooms and sauté until mushrooms are light brown. Season with sherry, salt and pepper. Top cornmeal mixture with mushroom mixture and robiola cheese cubes. Bake for 45 minutes. Set oven temperature to broil and lightly brown cheese. Cut into 8 wedges and serve immediately.

8 servings

BUTTERY MUSHROOM BREAD PUDDING

I served this simple yet incredibly savory dish at a sit-down dinner party and our guests loved it. I like using Amy's Organic Cream of Mushroom soup because it's chock full of mushroom flavor.

> *butter, softened*
> *6–8 slices (6 cups) bread*
> *1 can (14.1 ounces) Semi-Condensed Cream of Mushroom soup*
> *2 tablespoons cooking sherry*
> *⅓ cup minced fresh parsley*

Preheat oven to 350°F. Spread the butter evenly over the bread slices. Stack the slices and cube them. Place buttered bread cubes in a lightly oiled 2-quart casserole dish. In a medium bowl, combine the mushroom soup with the sherry and parsley. Pour mixture over bread cubes, cover and bake for 25 minutes or until bubbly. If desired, reset oven temperature to broil and brown the top. Serve immediately.

6 servings

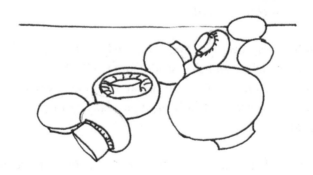

Pumpernickel Parmesan Polenta

This is a hearty side dish that I often serve for brunch. It goes well with sausage, steamed greens, stewed tomatoes or slices of fresh summer tomatoes. Allow pumpernickel slices to dry in a warm oven before crushing.

2 packages (16 ounces each) polenta
2 cups shredded cheddar cheese
⅓ cup minced fresh parsley
2 eggs
2½ cups half-and-half
½ teaspoon crushed red pepper flakes
½ cup fresh grated Parmesan cheese
2 sandwich-size slices dried-out pumpernickel bread, crushed

Preheat oven to 350°F. Cut polenta in half lengthwise and cut each half in half. Cut each of 8 pieces into 6 strips and coarsely chop strips. Place polenta in a 2-quart casserole dish and top with cheddar cheese and parsley. In a medium bowl, whisk eggs; add half-and-half and red pepper flakes. Pour mixture over polenta and bake for 30 minutes. Top polenta with Parmesan and crushed pumpernickel. Bake an additional 25 minutes. Serve immediately.

6 servings

CARAMELIZED CARROTS WITH KALAMATA OLIVES

Kalamata is the region in Greece that is famous for its production of olives as well as olive oils. These purple, almond-shaped fruits are hard to miss because of their beautiful color and pronounced salt and vinegar flavor.

3 tablespoons canola oil
1 pound carrots, peeled and cut about ¼-inch thick
8 cloves garlic, sliced
½ cup pitted and chopped Kalamata olives

Heat oil in a sauté pan over moderate heat, add carrots, and cook for about 15 minutes, stirring often. When carrots begin to caramelize and blacken slightly, add garlic. Reduce heat and cook an additional 5 minutes or until garlic is tender. Remove from heat and toss carrots with olives. Serve immediately.

4 servings

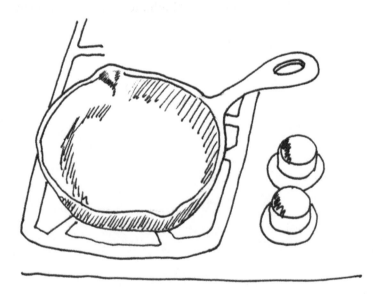

Nick's Potato Salad

Ironically, when I met the man who became my husband, he was the cook. One night, for dinner he served me thinly sliced potatoes that he had sprinkled with Lipton Onion Soup Mix and then baked until fork-tender. They were delicious. This recipe is a rendition of Nick's fabulous potatoes. The secret to the great-tasting flavor is in the timing of the tossing. The potatoes need to be warm when you toss them with the rest of the ingredients. Simply Organic makes a delicious French Onion Dip Mix.

2 pounds potatoes (peeling is a matter of preference)
1 package onion dip mix
½ cup olive oil
¼ cup minced fresh parsley

Cut potatoes into bite-size pieces and drop into a large pot of boiling water. Cover pot and cook potatoes until tender. Transfer potatoes to a medium serving bowl. In a small bowl, combine onion dip mix, olive oil and minced parsley; blend well. Pour the dressing over the still-warm potatoes and toss until fully incorporated. Serve immediately.

8 servings

BASIC BREAD STUFFING

I like to use several different types of bread when I make stuffing; a complementary trio is one third good-quality white bread, one third whole wheat bread and one third cornbread. It gives the stuffing a distinctly unusual flavor and a non-mushy texture. This is a good basic stuffing recipe. You can successfully add fillers like cranberries, apples, sausage, chestnuts, oysters and mushrooms. Baking the stuffing in a casserole dish or inside the bird is a matter of personal preference. Bread stuffing can be prepared in advance, but allow it to come to room temperature before heating.

½ cup (1 stick) butter
3 cups chopped celery
1½ cups chopped white onion
2 teaspoons salt
1 teaspoon paprika
several grindings of freshly ground black pepper
1 cup chicken broth
½ cup minced fresh parsley
15 cups bread, cut into bite-size cubes

Preheat oven to 350°F. In a medium pot over moderate heat, melt butter; add celery and onion and sauté for about 5–7 minutes or until fork-tender. Remove from heat. Add salt, paprika, black pepper, chicken broth and parsley. Stir to combine. Place bread cubes in a large bowl; toss with celery/onion/broth mixture and any additional fillers you choose. Transfer to a lightly oiled 4-quart casserole dish. Cover and bake for about 30 minutes. Remove cover and continue baking for 15 minutes. Serve immediately.

12 to 15 servings

CARROT AND LEEK GRATIN

A delicious side dish that's so versatile it can be served with beef, lamb, pork or chicken. Five tablespoons of horseradish may seem excessive, but it's what gives this dish a wonderful zesty flavor.

2 tablespoons butter
4 cups shredded carrots (about 6 medium)
2 cups sliced leeks (about 4–5 medium)
5 tablespoons prepared horseradish
1 teaspoon salt
a few grindings of freshly ground black pepper
1 cup heavy whipping cream
1 cup milk
2 eggs
⅓ cup dry bread crumbs
½ cup shredded white cheddar cheese

Preheat oven to 350°F. Lightly oil a 2-quart baking dish with cooking spray. In a large pot over moderate heat, melt butter and sauté carrots and leeks until tender, about 4–5 minutes. Remove from heat and stir in horseradish, salt and pepper. Transfer mixture to the baking dish. In a medium bowl, whisk together cream, milk and eggs. Pour over carrot/leek mixture and lightly stir to evenly distribute. Bake gratin uncovered for 30 minutes. In a small bowl, combine bread crumbs and cheese. Remove baking dish from oven and evenly distribute the bread crumb/cheese mixture on top. Bake uncovered for an additional 25 minutes. Serve immediately.

6 to 8 servings

BERRY NUTTY COUSCOUS

I developed this combination side dish for two of our vegetarian friends. It was a big hit, earned rave reviews taste-wise, and was very simple to prepare. Full of color and texture, this dish is as complementary to baked chicken and broiled fish as it is to tofu.

I use the Near East brand Couscous Mix with Toasted Pine Nuts.

> *2 boxes couscous (5.6 ounces each)*
> *1 cup crumbled feta cheese*
> *½ cup dried cranberries*
> *½ cup minced fresh parsley*

Cook couscous according to package directions. Transfer cooked couscous to a large serving bowl. Toss the couscous with crumbled feta cheese, dried cranberries and parsley. Serve at room temperature.

6 to 8 servings

GLOBE ARTICHOKES

Even if I lived in Castroville, California (the self-proclaimed Artichoke Center of the World), I don't think I'd tire of eating artichokes; they're at the top of my list of favorite foods. Just the word itself represents all things good to me: my husband's nickname for his lifelong friend Arthur is ART-tichoke, Marilyn Monroe was the first ever Miss Artichoke and, of course, there was our Norwich terrier/our love, Artichoke. I like to serve artichokes with my recipe for Artichoke Dip. We also love to dip the leaves in melted butter.

ARTICHOKE DIP
⅔ cup mayonnaise
4 teaspoons Worcestershire sauce
2 teaspoons Dijon-style mustard
2 teaspoons fresh lemon juice

In a medium bowl using a wire whisk, combine mayonnaise, Worcestershire sauce, mustard and lemon juice. Whisk until fully incorporated. Cover and refrigerate until serving time.

4 whole artichokes
Artichoke Dip or melted butter

Fill a large pot with cold water and bring to a boil. Wash artichokes by simply running them under water. With a sharp knife, trim stem, leaving a 1-inch stub. Cut off the top ¼-inch of the artichoke. With scissors, trim the sharp tips off each leaf. Place artichokes in boiling water, cover and reduce heat to medium (water should be dancing). Cook for about 40–50 minutes or until a fork inserted in the stem goes through easily. Drain artichokes and place in a casserole dish to accommodate, cover with tight fitting lid and let stand for about 30 minutes. Serve the artichokes warm and pass the Artichoke Dip or melted butter to your guests.

4 servings

CHINESE BROCCOLI

This is a tasty and colorful side dish that I like to serve with chicken, beef, fish or tofu. The secret to Chinese Broccoli is to not overcook the broccoli. Keep piercing it with a fork, and when it's just fork-tender, remove from heat and immediately transfer to a serving bowl. Broccoli stems can be tough, so before cooking, remove the outer layer with a paring knife and cut into bite-size pieces. While the broccoli is cooking, prepare the topping.

4 cups bite-size pieces of broccoli (florets and stems)
1 tablespoon toasted sesame oil
½ cup pine nuts
1 cup sliced yellow pepper
1–2 tablespoons reduced-sodium soy sauce
1 tablespoon black sesame seeds

In a large pot, steam broccoli until just fork-tender. Heat sesame oil in a large skillet over moderate heat, stir in pine nuts and cook for 1–2 minutes or until lightly browned, stirring frequently. Add yellow pepper and soy sauce and sauté for another 1–2 minutes. Remove from heat and pour over broccoli. Toss to evenly distribute the sauce. Sprinkle with black sesame seeds. Serve immediately.

4 servings

SAUERKRAUT

This is a family recipe that's been passed down from countless generations. I use Great Lakes Kraut Company's Silver Floss Traditional Shredded Sauerkraut.

32 ounces sauerkraut
1 large apple, peeled, cored and chopped
4 lean, raw pork ribs
several grindings of freshly ground black pepper

In a large pot, combine sauerkraut, apple, pork ribs and black pepper; cover contents with water and bring to a boil. Cover pot, reduce heat to simmer and cook for about 2–3 hours. Water may need to be added throughout the simmering process; sauerkraut should always be immersed in liquid. Allow sauerkraut to cool before storing overnight in the refrigerator.

Allow sauerkraut to come to room temperature before bringing to a gentle boil. Reduce heat, cover pot and simmer for a few hours. Remove pork bones before serving.

6 to 8 servings

Introducing

BREADS, BISCUITS, ROLLS

Throughout my youth, I remember coming home to the aroma of freshly baked bread. On school days, my mother would often begin making bread around lunchtime so that by the time we got home, the loaves were still warm from the oven and ready to eat. She didn't just make one particular recipe; she experimented with a variety of recipes, using different flours, grains and liquids (like milk, buttermilk, olive oil, etc.). Some loaves were textured and hearty; others were light and airy. Whatever kind she made, we would slather slices of that warm, freshly baked bread with butter, peanut butter or homemade jam.

Many years later, I decided I wanted to learn how to make bread. Serendipitously, my sister Kate (who had learned bread making from our mother) was visiting on that very day and in her straight-to-the-point style said, "Let's do it right now." As it turned out, this was the best way to teach me how to make bread: be afraid of nothing, jump right into the fire. Kate showed me bread making essentials, like how to proof yeast and knead dough, and though my first attempt was rather disastrous (the kitchen was a total mess, with flour everywhere) I persevered, sticky hands and all. While I was kneading (a process known to be very therapeutic), Kate and I reminisced about the unforgettable aroma that filled our childhood home, and our mouths watered as we recalled eating warm slices of bread spread with our favorite toppings. Determined to make those vivid memories a reality for both of us, I continued to knead that sticky mass of dough until it was smooth and elastic, exactly as my sister told me it should be.

Gratefully, the dough made it through its two separate risings, and yes, I kept peeking to make certain the dough was expanding. Allowing dough to rise is a critical step in bread making, so once it has risen properly and been placed into the oven to bake, you feel this great sense of accomplishment, even before a "real" loaf of bread comes out. So you can only imagine how I felt when I pulled my first loaf from the oven. I was thrilled beyond belief with my endeavor. Albeit the bread was a little lopsided and maybe not quite as high as my mother's version, to me it was perfect. Kate, Nick and I slathered warm slices with butter and it was delicious, almost as delicious as my mother's.

Bread Making Techniques
A Guide for Successful Bread Making

Making bread is not an exact science; as a rule, there is no right or wrong. I prefer to think of it as an art form, where each loaf is a one-of-a-kind masterpiece. Once you become accustomed to the basic practices involved in bread making, you'll probably find yourself baking quite often.

- Ingredients should be at room temperature.

- Yeast should be fresh (check the expiration date before using). Generally, yeast will not proof if the temperature of the liquid added is too cold or too hot. I use the inside of my wrist (an area that's sensitive to hot and cold) for testing the temperature of the liquid; it should be no hotter than what you would give a baby. Typically, yeast requires a warm, damp environment to proof, as well as the addition of honey or sugar. Proofing yeast is like watching a chemistry experiment; ingredients react to other ingredients. The process takes about 5–10 minutes, and the result should be a foamy and/or bubbly mixture.

- Dough can be quite temperamental and typically performs according to the weather conditions in your kitchen. Humidity makes for stickier dough, which means you'll need to add more flour while kneading; colder/dryer conditions will require less flour during this process. When adding flour during the kneading process, measurements are not exact; add flour until you have smooth, elastic dough. You will find many techniques for kneading dough; the perfect technique is the one that works best for you.

- Most bread dough requires at least two risings. During this process, dough should be in a warm environment, free of cold drafts. On top of a warm radiator, near something warming on the stove or on a warm day, in natural sunlight. You can also successfully allow the dough to rise in the oven. Set cold oven to 200°F. Let the oven preheat for 1 minute only. Turn oven off. Set covered dough in the oven, close the door and allow the dough to rise according to recipe directions. Rising times vary; on average, expect about one hour per rising.

- After a rising, you will always be asked to "punch down" the dough. Punching down is not so much about the act of punching as it is about the act of flattening. Using your fist or outstretched hand, push down the dough in order to deflate it.

For me, life seemed to come full circle on that day years ago, learning from my sister how to make bread from scratch successfully like our mother did, and then being doubly rewarded with all the precious and joyous childhood memories that eating warm, homemade bread evoked for both of us. Those memories are always with me each and every time I measure out flour to begin the bread making process. I think that's why I'm constantly encouraging people to experience bread making firsthand and encouraging those who may have had a less-than-stellar experience to give it another try. Baking bread from scratch is rewarding on a personal level, but nothing replaces the joy of sharing this culinary experience with the next generation of bread makers and creating your own family traditions.

BREADS, BISCUITS, ROLLS

Hot-Buttered-Rum Pumpkin Biscuits

Caraway Cheese Batter Bread

Dual-Seed Cornmeal Bread

Better Feather Biscuits

Focaccia

Golden Bread

Popovers

Oatmeal Rolls

Free-Form Country Bread

Crunchy Whole-Seed Bread

Radish Bread with Caraway Seeds

Vegetable Flat Cakes with Basil Cream

HOT-BUTTERED-RUM PUMPKIN BISCUITS

When a group of my friends first tasted these amber-colored square morsels hot from the oven, the response was an overwhelming "Wow!" We slathered them with Autumn Orange Butter (see page 46) and ate the whole batch.

This recipe is one of many in *Tasting the Seasons* that includes The Spice Hunter Winter Sippers Hot Buttered Rum Mix. This recipe calls for 100% pure pumpkin and not pumpkin pie filling.

> *2 cups unbleached all-purpose flour*
> *⅓ cup yellow cornmeal*
> *2 tablespoons Winter Sippers Hot Buttered Rum Mix*
> *1 tablespoon baking powder*
> *½ teaspoon salt*
> *⅓ cup canola oil*
> *1 cup pure pumpkin*
> *½ cup heavy cream*
> *2 tablespoons honey*

Preheat oven to 400°F. In a large bowl, combine flour, cornmeal, Winter Sippers Hot Buttered Rum Mix, baking powder and salt. Drizzle ⅓ cup canola oil over flour mixture and toss with a fork, allowing flour to absorb oil. In a medium bowl, combine pumpkin, cream and honey; mix until well blended. Add to flour mixture and knead dough until ingredients are combined (dough will be sticky). Sprinkle work surface with flour and form dough into a rough 9-inch square. Cut into 16 squares and place on a greased baking sheet. Bake until golden brown, about 20 minutes. Serve immediately.

16 biscuits

CARAWAY CHEESE BATTER BREAD

Fans of caraway are going to adore this dark-crusted, moist bread. These aromatic and flavorful seeds add a wonderfully distinctive taste to this cheese bread, and while Swiss works well, I also recommend experimenting with different cheeses. Try cheddar and Monterey Jack for equally great results.

1 package active dry yeast
2 tablespoons sugar
1¼ cups warm water
2 cups shredded Swiss cheese
2 tablespoons olive oil
2 teaspoons salt
3 tablespoons caraway seeds
2⅔ cups unbleached all-purpose flour

In a large mixing bowl, dissolve the yeast with sugar and warm water. Allow the yeast to proof in a warm, draft-free spot. Add cheese, olive oil, salt, caraway seeds and 2 cups of flour to the yeast mixture. Using an electric mixer, beat on medium speed for about 2 minutes. Add remaining ⅔ cup flour and stir until incorporated. Transfer to a floured surface and knead until smooth, about 3–5 minutes. Place in an oiled 9 x 5 x 3-inch loaf pan. Cover with kitchen towel. Let rise until doubled in bulk, about 1½ hours.

Preheat oven to 375°F. Bake bread for about 45 minutes or until loaf sounds hollow when tapped on the top and bottom. Cool the loaf on wire rack before serving.

One loaf

DUAL-SEED CORNMEAL BREAD

Full of crunch and texture, this is a delicious loaf. It's marvelous when simply toasted and keeps well for a few days when refrigerated.

To toast millet, bake in a 350°F oven or toaster oven until lightly browned. Watch closely; there's a narrow window between toasted and burned.

> *2 packages active dry yeast*
> *1½ cups warm water*
> *1 tablespoon sugar*
> *3 teaspoons salt*
> *½ cup cornmeal*
> *1 cup warm milk*
> *¼ cup light brown sugar*
> *½ cup millet seed, toasted*
> *½ cup whole flax seeds, ground*
> *4–5 cups unbleached all-purpose flour*

In a large bowl, proof yeast with ½ cup warm water and sugar. In a medium saucepan, bring remaining 1 cup of water to a boil. Add 1 teaspoon salt and cornmeal. Lower heat to a simmer and cook for 1 minute, stirring vigorously. Cool mixture for about 5 minutes. Transfer the mixture to the bowl with yeast the mixture. Add remaining salt, milk, brown sugar, toasted millet and ground flax seeds; stir until well combined. Add flour, 1 cup at a time, stirring well after each addition. When the mixture begins to pull away from the sides of the bowl, transfer to a floured surface and knead for about 10 minutes or until smooth and elastic. Lightly coat a large bowl with oil, transfer the dough into the bowl and coat the dough on all surfaces with oil. Cover with a kitchen towel and let the dough rise in a warm, draft-free place until double in bulk, about 1 hour.

Punch dough down, cut in half and shape into 2 rounds. Place each in a 9 x 5 x 3-inch loaf pan, cover both pans with a kitchen towel and let the dough rise until double in bulk, about 1 hour.

Preheat oven to 425°F. Bake loaves for 10 minutes. Lower temperature to 350°F and bake an additional 20–25 minutes or until loaves are light brown and sound hollow when tapped on the top and bottom. Allow the loaves to cool before slicing.

Two loaves

BETTER FEATHER BISCUITS

My grandmother made the most amazing biscuits—feathery, fluffy and soft. She made them with lard, a fashionable cooking ingredient in her day. My mother introduced me to an organic, non-hydrogenated, trans fat-free vegetable shortening, and I created a version of my grandmother's delicious biscuits.

> *1 package active dry yeast*
> *¼ teaspoon sugar*
> *2 tablespoons warm water*
> *2½ cups unbleached all-purpose flour*
> *⅛ cup sugar*
> *1 teaspoon salt*
> *½ cup vegetable shortening*
> *1 cup buttermilk*

In a small bowl, dissolve yeast, sugar and warm water; let proof for about 5 minutes. In a large bowl, combine 2½ cups flour, sugar and salt. With the tips of your fingers or a pastry blender, cut the shortening in until the flour mixture forms pieces the size of peas. Add the yeast mixture and buttermilk to the flour mixture, stirring until combined. The dough will be sticky and slightly wet. Transfer to a bowl that has been lightly coated with oil, cover and refrigerate overnight.

Turn dough out onto a lightly floured surface. Roll until dough is ½-inch thick, and cut with a 2¼-inch biscuit cutter. Arrange biscuits on 2 lightly oiled baking sheets. Cover the biscuits with kitchen towels and let rise for 1½ hours.

Preheat oven to 400°F. Bake biscuits for about 15 minutes. Switch baking sheets halfway through cooking time to ensure even baking. Serve immediately.

24 biscuits

FOCACCIA

Focaccia is an Italian flatbread with a crispy crust and a chewy-yet-soft interior. I've been making bread for decades, and this is one of the most popular. This focaccia is delicious sans toppings, but many ingredients can be successfully added to the loaf; topping amounts are a matter of personal preference.

OPTIONAL ADD-ON IDEAS: Thyme, sage, basil, oregano and rosemary, black olives, fresh ground black pepper, grated cheese, fresh tomatoes, caramelized onions, roasted vegetables.

> *5½ cups unbleached all-purpose flour*
> *¼ cup sugar*
> *1 package active dry yeast*
> *1 tablespoon kosher salt*
> *2½ cups cold water*
> *8 tablespoons olive oil*

In a large bowl, combine flour, sugar, yeast, 1 tablespoon salt and water. Mix ingredients with your hands. The dough will be very sticky. Knead the dough for about 3 minutes. Let it rest for about 5 minutes. Knead for another 2–3 minutes. The dough will be somewhat smooth, but still very sticky.

Place dough in another large bowl and add 1 tablespoon of olive oil; turn dough to coat on all surfaces. Grab a large portion of the dough with one hand, hold it above the bowl and allow it to stretch out until it doubles in size. Repeat this process 3 more times. Drizzle 1 tablespoon of olive oil over the dough. Wrap the bowl with plastic wrap, cover bowl with a kitchen towel and refrigerate overnight.

About 3–4 hours before you plan to bake the bread, line the bottom and overlap the sides of an 11½ x 16½ x 1-inch, rimmed baking sheet with parchment paper. Coat the paper with 2 tablespoons olive oil. Transfer dough to the parchment paper using a rubber spatula. Drizzle the dough with 2 tablespoons olive oil. Starting in the center of the dough, splay your fingers and make indentations over the surface of the dough, creating hollows as the dough is moved down and out toward the edges of the baking pan. When dough begins to resist, let it rest for about 20 minutes.

Drizzle another 2 tablespoons of olive oil over the dough and repeat the last process until the dough nearly reaches the edges of the baking pan. Dough doesn't have to be snug in each corner;

it will do this naturally during the next rising. Cover the dough loosely with plastic wrap, then top the plastic wrap with a kitchen towel. Place the pan on a wire rack and allow dough to rise for about 2–3 hours.

About 30 minutes prior to baking, preheat oven to 475°F. Sprinkle focaccia with kosher salt or desired toppings and place the baking pan in the middle of oven. Reduce temperature to 450°F and bake for 15–20 minutes or until golden brown. Cool for about 10 minutes before cutting.

One flatbread

GOLDEN BREAD

I love to serve this for breakfast with poached eggs and fried green tomatoes. It's also delicious when topped with assorted roasted vegetables. Golden Bread is a good keeper and can be fried all at once (in batches) or as needed.

2 cups chicken broth
2 cups water
1 vegetable bouillon cube
1 teaspoon salt
2 cups cornmeal
canola oil for frying

In a large pot, bring chicken broth and water to a boil. Stir in vegetable cube and salt, allowing cube to dissolve before slowly adding the cornmeal. Stir the mixture constantly with a wooden spoon. When mixture begins to thicken and splatter, reduce heat to medium. Cook an additional 5–10 minutes or until thick. Remove from heat and spoon mixture into a 9½ x 5½ x 3-inch baking dish. Allow the mixture to cool before refrigerating overnight.

Slice polenta into ¼–½-inch slices or desired thickness. Heat oil in a large skillet over medium heat and cook slices until golden and slightly brown on each side. Serve immediately.

8 servings

POPOVERS

It is hard to believe that with only four ingredients and a mere fifteen minutes of baking time, you can have a delicious, crusty-on-the-outside, soft-on-the-inside popover. These are great on their own with butter and jam or as an accompaniment to soup. If you want a savory, flavored popover, simply add half a teaspoon of your favorite dried herb. If you don't have a popover pan, you can use a 12-cup muffin tin. Simply fill alternating cups so that the popovers have room to "pop over."

> *½ cup milk*
> *2 eggs*
> *1 tablespoon canola oil*
> *¾ cup unbleached all-purpose flour*

Place oven rack in lowest position and preheat oven to 450°F. In a medium bowl, whisk together milk, eggs and 1 tablespoon canola oil; add flour and whisk until mixture is smooth. Generously oil six muffin cups; place muffin tin in oven for 3 minutes. Remove tin from oven and immediately spoon batter into cups, filling ¾ full. Reduce oven temperature to 350°F and bake popovers for 15 minutes. Serve immediately.

6 popovers

OATMEAL ROLLS

These rolls are best eaten hot from the oven slathered with butter.

> *2 cups quick cooking oats*
> *2 cups milk*
> *1 package active dry yeast*
> *¾ cup warm water*
> *1 teaspoon sugar*
> *¼ cup olive oil*
> *1 teaspoon salt*
> *4 cups unbleached all-purpose flour*

In a large bowl, combine quick cooking oats and milk. Cover and let the mixture stand at room temperature for about 2 hours. In a small bowl, dissolve yeast in water, add sugar and allow the mixture to proof. Add yeast mixture to milk/oatmeal mixture. Add olive oil and salt, and stir until well-combined. Add flour 1 cup at a time. When dough begins to pull away from the sides of the bowl (after about the third cup), transfer to a floured surface. Knead dough until it is smooth and elastic, adding additional flour as needed. Knead for about 7–10 minutes.

Lightly coat a large bowl with oil, place dough into bowl and turn dough to coat all surfaces. Cover with a kitchen towel and let rise in a warm, draft-free place until doubled in bulk, about 1 hour.

Punch dough down and then transfer to lightly floured work surface. Roll to 1-inch thickness and cut into 32 rolls using a 2¼-inch biscuit cutter. Place onto 2 prepared baking sheets, parchment lined or oiled. Cover rolls with a kitchen towel and let rise for about 1 hour.

Preheat oven to 425°F. Bake the rolls for 18–20 minutes, switching baking sheets halfway through the baking time. Serve immediately.

32 rolls

Free-Form Country Bread

A free-form loaf is one that is not baked in a bread pan. As yeast breads go, this dough is simple, quick and baker-friendly. With just two risings at about one hour each, you can easily prepare this delicious bread and have it ready in time for lunch.

> 1 package active dry yeast
> 1 teaspoon sugar
> 2⅔ cups warm water
> 1½ teaspoons salt
> 3½–5 cups unbleached all-purpose flour

Combine yeast, sugar and ⅓ cup warm water in a large bowl; stir until yeast dissolves. Proof yeast for about 10–15 minutes. After yeast has proofed, add salt and remaining 2⅓ cups warm water to the bowl. Add 2 cups of flour and stir well. Continue adding flour, about ½ cup at a time, stirring well after each addition, until dough begins to pull away from the sides of the bowl. Turn out onto a lightly floured surface. Knead until bread is smooth and elastic, adding flour as needed to keep dough from sticking. Lightly coat a large bowl with oil, transfer the dough to the bowl and coat all surfaces of the dough with oil. Cover with a kitchen towel and allow dough to rise for about 1 hour.

After the first rising, punch dough down and place on a rimmed baking sheet that has been lightly coated with cooking spray and dusted with cornmeal. Cover with a kitchen towel and let rise for about 1 hour.

Preheat oven to 450°F. Bake bread for 10 minutes. Reduce heat to 350°F and bake an additional 20 minutes or until bread sounds hollow when tapped on the top and bottom. Allow the loaf to cool before slicing.

One loaf

CRUNCHY WHOLE-SEED BREAD

This is a nutritious loaf made with Salba, a 100% natural whole food that is gluten-free and rich in fiber, omega-3 fatty acids, antioxidants, vitamins and minerals. Salba comes in whole and ground seed; I prefer the whole seed. It's what gives this bread its pleasing, crunchy texture.

> *1 package active dry yeast*
> *1 teaspoon sugar*
> *2⅔ cups warm water*
> *1½ teaspoons salt*
> *½ cup whole seed Salba*
> *3½–5 cups unbleached all-purpose flour*

In a large bowl, combine yeast, sugar and ⅓ cup warm water; stir mixture until yeast dissolves. Proof yeast for about 10–15 minutes. Add salt and remaining 2⅓ cups warm water. Add Salba and 1 cup flour, then continue adding flour 1 cup at a time, stirring well after each addition. When dough begins to pull away from the sides of the bowl, turn out onto a lightly floured surface. Knead until dough is smooth and elastic, adding flour as needed to keep the dough from sticking. Lightly coat a large bowl with oil, coat all surfaces of dough, cover bowl with a kitchen towel and allow the dough to rise for about 1 hour.

Punch dough down and place on a rimmed baking pan that has been lightly coated with oil and dusted with cornmeal. Cover dough with kitchen towel and let rise for another hour.

Preheat oven to 450°F. Bake bread for 10 minutes; reduce heat to 350°F and bake an additional 20 minutes or until loaf sounds hollow when tapped on the top and bottom. Allow the bread to cool before slicing.

One loaf

RADISH BREAD WITH CARAWAY SEEDS

This dough is soft, pliable and very easy to handle, making it a good recipe for those less experienced with yeast bread.

> *1 package active dry yeast*
> *1 teaspoon sugar*
> *1½ cups water*
> *2 teaspoons salt*
> *2 teaspoons caraway seeds*
> *1 cup unpeeled and shredded radishes*
> *4–4½ cups unbleached all-purpose flour*

In a large bowl, combine yeast with sugar and ½ cup warm water; stir until yeast has dissolved. Allow yeast to proof in a warm, draft-free place for about 15 minutes or until foamy. Stir in remaining water, salt, caraway seeds, radishes and 1 cup of flour. Add remaining flour, 1 cup at a time, stirring well after each addition. When dough begins to pull away from the sides of the bowl, transfer to a floured surface and knead for about 5–8 minutes. Add more flour to keep the dough from sticking to the surface. Knead until dough is smooth and elastic. Lightly coat a bowl with oil, transfer the dough into the bowl and coat the dough on all surfaces with oil. Cover bowl with a kitchen towel and allow dough to rise in a warm, draft-free spot until it doubles in bulk, about 1 hour.

Punch dough down, lightly coat with flour and shape into a round. Coat a 9 x 5 x 3-inch bread pan with oil, transfer dough, cover with a kitchen towel and allow to rise in a warm, draft-free spot until it doubles in bulk, about 1 hour.

Preheat oven to 375°F. Bake bread for 30 minutes or until the loaf sounds hollow when tapped on the top and the bottom. Allow the bread to cool before slicing.

One loaf

VEGETABLE FLAT CAKES WITH BASIL CREAM

The recipe for these tasty, colorful, pancake-style treats was yet another positive result of an experiment with food on hand. For a delicious meal, serve with either Home-Harvested Gazpacho or Cold Crab and Corn Soup (see Index for recipes).

1 cup sour cream
1 cup fresh basil leaves, minced
½ teaspoon salt
a few dashes Tabasco sauce or hot pepper sauce
1½ cups unbleached all-purpose flour
2 teaspoons baking powder
½ teaspoon salt
1½ cups unpeeled, shredded zucchini
½ cup finely chopped red pepper
1 cup shredded Swiss cheese
1 egg
1 cup milk
canola oil for frying

In a medium bowl, combine sour cream, basil leaves, salt and Tabasco or hot pepper sauce. Mix until well blended. In a large bowl combine flour, baking powder and salt. Add zucchini, red pepper and Swiss cheese. In a medium bowl, whisk egg with milk. Add to flour/vegetable mixture and combine using swift strokes. Coat a large skillet with canola oil and heat over medium-high heat. To ensure the pan is hot enough to cook the flat cakes, sprinkle oil with water, and when it sizzles, spoon about a ¼ cup of the mixture into the skillet, cooking three flat cakes at a time. Cook for about 2 minutes on each side or until light brown. Serve immediately with basil cream.

About 12 flat cakes

Introducing

SWEET ENDINGS

My grandparents ate dessert every night after dinner and sometimes after lunch as well. Dessert was typically pudding, custard, made-from-scratch tapioca (the kind that was soaked overnight before cooking), assorted canned fruit, and homemade cake and pie (the latter two were reserved for weekends and special occasions). The creamier, softer desserts and canned fruit were usually accompanied by a cookie and eaten while watching *The Lawrence Welk Show*. Oh, those idyllic moments when I sat with my grandmother and grandfather on their davenport in front of the large, boxy television set, partaking of life's sweetness while watching their beloved Lawrence Welk. I was too young to realize how simple and beautiful their lives were, but I am extraordinarily grateful for all of my memories.

Fast forward to the sweet endings my mother prepared. In our house, dessert wasn't served as frequently as it was at my grandparents' house, especially the kind of dessert that would absorb most of an afternoon for my mother. Those kinds of desserts were saved for special occasions, and oh, did we kids relish those occasions and the delicious desserts she made! My mother always made a point of telling us that she was not a perfect baker; we, in turn, always chimed back that whatever she baked tasted perfect. And it was true. Her desserts were charmingly lopsided, and we loved her homespun decorations. But what we loved most of all was the never-to-be-duplicated-unless-it's-homemade taste of everything she lovingly made.

In this section you'll find a sampling of some of the desserts my grandparents enjoyed. My version of their pudding is vegan and made using tofu, and every time I eat it, I wonder what they would think of the main ingredient. Other recipes are representative of desserts my mother served, like Rolled Chocolate Pudding Cake or the ever-popular Baked Alaska. Of course, many of the desserts you'll find are in keeping with my personal philosophy, using (and sometimes disguising) fruits and vegetables, as in Parsnip Baby Cakes with Ginger Icing and Rhubarb Cake. And finally, some sweet endings are simply downright decadent, like Caramel Centered Chocolate Cookies and the can't-stop-eating Oh, my! Shortbread.

SWEET ENDINGS

Baked Alaska

Blueberry Bars

Cinnamon Ginger Cookies

Hazelnut Fudge Truffles

Rolled Chocolate Pudding Cake

Pumpkin Roll-Up Cake with Cream Cheese Filling

Caramel-Centered Chocolate Cookies

Chocolate Pistachio Cream Cake

Ginger Cake with Toffee Sauce

Chilean Carica and Cardamom Frozen Yogurt

Parsnip Baby Cakes with Ginger Icing

Crispy Creamy Apple Turnovers

Whirled Peaches with Amaretto

Creamy Chocolate Pudding

Very Fruity Pudding

Rhubarb Cake

Summer's Berry Bread Pudding

Strawberry Cobbler Cake

Coconut Lime Cake

Almond Shortbread

Peach Cake

Oh, my! Shortbread

BAKED ALASKA

When I presented this at a sit-down dinner party we hosted, the conversation immediately turned to how this beautiful dessert evoked fond memories of Julia Child. Whether or not Baked Alaska takes you back to the 50s, this dessert is as unforgettable now as it was back then.

You will need a kitchen torch for this recipe. To toast slivered almonds, place them on a baking sheet (a toaster oven tray works perfectly) in a 350° oven until brown. Watch carefully to make sure they don't burn. Beat the egg whites just before serving.

> *1 quart frozen yogurt or ice cream, semi-softened*
> *2 egg whites*
> *¼ cup sugar*
> *⅛ teaspoon cream of tartar*
> *chocolate sauce (see page 35)*
> *⅓ cup slivered almonds, toasted*

Line a 1-quart mold, or eight ½-cup molds, with plastic wrap. Allow enough wrap to hang over the sides so that there's enough to cover the mold(s) once filled with frozen yogurt or ice cream. Fill mold(s), cover and freeze until a few minutes before you're going to prepare the egg whites.

In a medium bowl, beat egg whites with an electric mixer on high speed. Gradually add sugar and continue beating until egg whites form stiff peaks; add cream of tartar and continue to beat until glossy. Drizzle chocolate sauce over 1 serving platter or 8 dessert plates. Invert mold(s) onto platter or individual plates. Working quickly, top the molds with the meringue and spread just as if you were icing a cake. Form peaks using a knife or the back of a spoon. Using a kitchen torch, lightly brown the meringue, and sprinkle with almonds. Serve immediately.

8 servings

BLUEBERRY BARS

Everyone loves these sweet, buttery, blueberry bars.

1 cup (2 sticks) butter, softened
⅔ cup sugar
2 cups unbleached all-purpose flour
½ cup (1 stick) butter
⅔ cup sugar
16 ounces frozen blueberries
3 tablespoons unbleached all-purpose flour

Preheat oven to 350°F. In a food processor, pulse butter a few times and add sugar ⅓ of a cup at a time, pulsing after each addition. Add flour 1 cup at a time, pulsing after each addition. When the mixture has come together and is the consistency of cookie dough, transfer to a lightly oiled 13 x 9-inch baking pan. Press dough evenly into baking pan and bake for 20 minutes.

Melt butter in a medium saucepan over moderate heat. Add sugar and blueberries. When blueberries have released their juice, whisk in flour 1 tablespoon at a time. Stir until well blended. Pour blueberry topping evenly over crust and bake for an additional 25 minutes. Let bars cool completely before cutting into squares.

Twenty-four 2-inch bars

CINNAMON GINGER COOKIES

Cinnamon, cloves and ginger make these cookies reminiscent of gingersnaps. Adding coarsely ground flax seeds gives the cookies an unexpected yet delightful crunch.

1 cup whole flax seeds, coarsely ground
2 cups unbleached all-purpose flour
2 teaspoons baking soda
1½ teaspoons ground cinnamon
½ teaspoon ground cloves
½ teaspoon ground ginger
½ teaspoon salt
1 cup sugar, plus an additional 2–3 tablespoons
½ cup apple butter
¼ cup molasses
2 tablespoons canola oil
1 egg

Preheat oven to 350°F. Lightly oil rimmed baking sheets with cooking spray. In a large bowl, combine ½ cup flax seeds, flour, baking soda, cinnamon, cloves, ginger, salt and 1 cup sugar. Mix until well blended. In a medium bowl, whisk apple butter, molasses, canola oil and egg, and whisk until well blended. Add liquid ingredients to dry ingredients and combine until fully incorporated. Place the remaining flax seeds in a small bowl. Place 2–3 tablespoons sugar in another small bowl. Lightly coat your hands with canola oil. Take about 1 tablespoon dough and shape into a ball. First roll each ball in flax seeds and then roll in sugar. Place on baking sheet about 2 inches apart and bake for about 12 minutes or until golden. Cool on baking sheet for 2 minutes before transferring to a wire rack to cool completely.

About 3½ dozen cookies

Hazelnut Fudge Truffles

This combination of ingredients was originally intended as icing for a Yule cake I was making over the holidays. However, the cake turned out to be so pleasingly attractive that I decided not to guild the lily by icing it.

½ cup (1 stick) butter
4 ounces unsweetened chocolate
¼ cup heavy whipping cream
1 teaspoon vanilla
2 cups confectioners' sugar
1 cup finely chopped hazelnuts

Melt butter and chocolate in a medium pan over low heat and stir until well combined. Whisk in cream and vanilla. Add confectioners' sugar ¼ cup at a time, stirring well after each addition. Once you have added all the sugar, the mixture will suddenly come together. Allow fudge truffle mixture to cool before refrigerating overnight.

To form chocolate into balls, allow fudge truffle mixture to come to room temperature. The fudge should be relatively hard, but pliable enough to roll into balls. Measure out a heaping teaspoon of the mixture and roll between the palms of your hands until you have a smooth ball. Place balls on a large platter with space in between truffles. Sprinkle with chopped hazelnuts. Refrigerate for a few hours until truffles harden.

About 40 truffles

ROLLED CHOCOLATE PUDDING CAKE

This cake is a real crowd-pleaser and it's surprisingly simple to assemble. Kozy Shack brand makes a delicious, homemade Chocolate All Natural Pudding.

¾ cup unbleached all-purpose flour
½ teaspoon baking soda
½ teaspoon baking powder
¼ teaspoon salt
¼ cup cocoa powder
¾ cup sugar
3 eggs
⅔ cup chocolate pudding
8 ounces light cream cheese, softened
6 tablespoons butter, softened
1 cup confectioners' sugar
1 teaspoon vanilla

Preheat oven to 350°F. Lightly oil a 17½ x 11½-inch rimmed baking sheet, and then line the pan with parchment paper. Lightly coat parchment paper with oil and lightly dust with flour. Set prepared pan aside. In a medium bowl, combine ¾ cup flour, baking soda, baking powder, salt, cocoa powder and sugar. In a large bowl, beat eggs with electric mixer, add chocolate pudding and beat until well combined. Add flour mixture and beat on medium speed until incorporated. Spread batter evenly into pan (it will seem like there's not enough batter, but there is) and bake for 10 minutes.

Generously dust a kitchen cloth (the cloth should be a little larger than the size of the cake) with confectioners' sugar. Immediately remove cake (lifting it up by the parchment paper) from baking pan and carefully flip cake onto prepared kitchen towel. Gently pull off parchment paper. Starting at the narrow end, roll the cake with the towel. Don't worry if the cake breaks as you're rolling it up; it won't be noticeable. Cool cake on a wire rack for 30 minutes.

In a large bowl, beat cream cheese with butter until well combined. Add confectioners' sugar and vanilla and beat for about 2 minutes on medium speed. Carefully unroll cake and spread filling evenly over entire cake (while still on towel). Gently re-roll cake (without towel), and cover with plastic wrap. Refrigerate for several hours or overnight prior to serving. Transfer cake to a serving platter, dust with confectioners' sugar and cut into slices about 1-inch thick.

10 to 12 servings

Pumpkin Roll-Up Cake
with Cream Cheese Filling

The weekend prior to Thanksgiving, our Cooking Club gathered for dinner to celebrate the holiday. My contribution was dessert, and thoughts of making a traditional pumpkin pie just didn't appeal to me. Enter The Spice Hunter Winter Sippers Hot Buttered Rum Mix and voilà! This delicious dessert was created.

Winter Sippers Hot Buttered Rum Mix is available during the Fall/Winter season and can be found in Whole Foods Market and most specialty grocery stores or online. Make certain to purchase 100% pure pumpkin and not pumpkin pie filling. Use the leftover pumpkin for Hot-Buttered-Rum Pumpkin Pancakes (see page 63).

> ¾ cup unbleached all-purpose flour
> ½ teaspoon baking soda
> ½ teaspoon baking powder
> ¼ teaspoon salt
> ½ cup Winter Sippers Hot Buttered Rum Mix
> ½ cup sugar
> 3 eggs
> ⅔ cup pure pumpkin
> 8 ounces light cream cheese, softened
> 6 tablespoons butter, softened
> 1 cup confectioners' sugar
> 1 teaspoon vanilla

Preheat oven to 350°F. Lightly oil a 17½ x 11½-inch rimmed baking sheet, and then line the pan with parchment paper. Lightly coat parchment paper with oil and then lightly dust with flour. Set prepared pan aside. In a medium bowl, combine flour, baking soda, baking powder, salt, Winter Sippers Hot Buttered Rum Mix and sugar. In a large bowl, beat eggs with electric mixer, add pumpkin and beat until well combined.

Add flour mixture and beat on medium speed until incorporated. Spread batter evenly into pan (it will seem like there's not enough batter, but there is) and bake cake for 10 minutes.

Generously dust a kitchen cloth (the cloth should be a little larger than the size of the cake) with confectioners' sugar. Immediately remove cake (lifting it up by the parchment paper) from baking pan and carefully flip cake onto prepared kitchen towel. Gently pull off parchment paper. Starting at the narrow end, roll the cake with the towel. Don't worry if the cake breaks as you're rolling it up, in the end, it won't be noticeable. Cool cake on a wire rack for 30 minutes.

In a large bowl, beat cream cheese with butter until well combined; add confectioners'sugar and vanilla and beat for about 2 minutes on medium speed. Carefully unroll cake and spread filling evenly over entire cake (while still on towel). Gently re-roll cake (without towel), and cover with plastic wrap. Refrigerate for several hours or overnight prior to serving. Transfer cake to a serving platter and cut into slices about 1-inch thick.

10 to 12 servings

CARAMEL-CENTERED CHOCOLATE COOKIES

Annabelle Creamer is the talent behind this recipe. We met Annabelle when Nick was scouting a condominium for a client. When we arrived for a tour of her apartment, she was busy making food for a luncheon she was hosting the following day. I don't recall which came first, Annabelle recognizing me from the cover of my cookbook, *This Book Cooks*, or me spotting my cookbook on a shelf in her kitchen. It doesn't really matter which came first; an instant bond was formed, and we sat and shared our passion for all things food. Shortly after we met, Annabelle invited us to a Julia Child-style dinner party where she served these delicious cookies.

1 cup (2 sticks) butter, softened
1 cup firmly packed brown sugar
1 cup sugar
2 eggs
2 teaspoons vanilla
2¼ cups unbleached all-purpose flour
¾ cup cocoa
1 teaspoon baking soda
1 package (12 ounces) Rolo chewy caramel candy
1 tablespoon sugar

In a large bowl, beat butter until creamy. Gradually add brown and white sugars and beat until well combined. Add eggs one at a time, beating until well blended; add vanilla and blend. In another large bowl, combine flour, cocoa and baking soda. Add to butter mixture and stir until fully combined. Refrigerate dough for 1 hour or preferably overnight. Allow the dough to come to room temperature before forming cookies. Dough should yield slightly to touch.

Preheat oven to 375°F. Gently press 1 tablespoon dough around each piece of Rolo candy and form into a ball. Dip one side of the ball in sugar and place dipped balls (sugar side up) on an ungreased baking sheet about 2 inches apart. Bake for about 7–8 minutes. Let cookies sit for 1 minute before transferring to a wire rack to cool.

About 4 to 4½ dozen cookies

CHOCOLATE PISTACHIO CREAM CAKE

For the most part, I'm a no-frills baker, a practice I picked up from my mother. Whenever she baked, she always said, "It doesn't look picture perfect," and we children always finished the sentence with, "but it tastes perfectly delicious." For her 82nd birthday party, I wanted to share a wonderful combination that I'd eaten for years in ice cream form, by featuring these ingredients in cake form. Needless to say, this dessert was a huge success, as was the special rendition of "Happy Birthday, dear Mom-Mom," as sung by my brother's three children, Connor, Garrett and Keelinn.

Chill the bowl and beaters in the refrigerator for at least 2 hours before whipping the cream. The cake can be assembled and refrigerated until it is ready to serve. Allow the cake to come to room temperature before serving.

> ½ cup canola oil
> 1 cup water
> ½ cup buttermilk
> 4 tablespoons cocoa powder
> 2 cups sugar
> 2 cups unbleached all-purpose flour
> 2 eggs
> 1 teaspoon baking soda
> 1 teaspoon vanilla

Preheat oven to 350°F. In a medium saucepan, whisk canola oil, water, buttermilk, cocoa powder and sugar until well blended. Bring mixture to a boil, remove from heat, and whisk in flour ½ cup at a time, whisking well after each addition. Whisk in eggs, baking soda and vanilla. Lightly oil two 8-inch round cake pans and pour batter into prepared pans. Bake for 15–20 minutes or until toothpick inserted in center of cake comes out clean. Allow the cakes to cool completely.

PISTACHIO CREAM
½ cup raw pistachios
2 teaspoons canola oil
¼ cup sugar
½ cup heavy whipping cream

In a food processor or blender, grind nuts until fine. Slowly drizzle in canola oil, add sugar, and mix until fully incorporated. In a medium bowl, beat cream on medium speed until cream thickens slightly. Increase speed and beat until soft peaks form, but watch closely: if you over-beat the cream, it will turn to butter. Fold in pistachio mixture and combine until completely incorporated. Transfer one cake layer to a cake platter. Spread pistachio mixture over top of layer, leaving a 1-inch border. Top with second layer of cake. Cover cake and refrigerate until icing is ready.

CHOCOLATE ICING

6 ounces semi-sweet chocolate
½ cup (1 stick) butter, softened
1 cup confectioners' sugar
2 teaspoons vanilla
¼ cup milk

In a medium pan, melt chocolate and butter over low heat. Remove from heat and add confectioners' sugar. Beat until smooth. Beat in vanilla, slowly drizzle in milk, and beat until fully combined. Keep at room temperature until the mixture has cooled and has the consistency of icing. Spread chocolate icing evenly over top and sides of cake.

12 to 14 servings

GINGER CAKE WITH TOFFEE SAUCE

This is a dessert the British are famous for serving. It's a perfect treat for a cold winter's night.

> *1 cup pitted and chopped dates*
> *1¼ cups water*
> *1 teaspoon baking soda*
> *4 tablespoons butter, softened*
> *⅔ cup sugar*
> *2 eggs*
> *1 teaspoon vanilla*
> *1¼ cups unbleached all-purpose flour*
> *1 teaspoon baking powder*
> *1 teaspoon ground ginger*
> *½ teaspoon cinnamon*
> *¼ teaspoon ground cloves*
> *¼ teaspoon salt*
> *vanilla custard, ice cream or frozen yogurt*

In a medium saucepan over medium heat, combine the dates and water. Simmer for about 10–15 minutes or until dates are soft. Add baking soda (mixture will foam) and stir until combined.

Preheat oven to 350F°. In a large bowl, with an electric beater, cream butter and slowly add sugar. Add eggs one at a time and beat until mixture is pale and fluffy. Add vanilla. In a medium bowl, combine flour, baking powder, ground ginger, cinnamon, cloves and salt. Slowly add dry ingredients to butter mixture. Mix until well combined. Fold in date mixture. Spoon batter into a greased 9-inch round cake pan and bake for 30 minutes or until toothpick inserted in center of cake comes out clean.

TOFFEE SAUCE
1½ cups sugar
¼ cup (½ stick) butter
1 cup heavy cream

In a large saucepan over medium heat, cook ½ cup sugar, stirring constantly with a wooden spoon until sugar turns light brown. Add remaining sugar, ½ cup at a time, allowing each batch to turn light brown. Cook sugar until chestnut brown (cooking the sugar takes about 15 minutes and you must stir it constantly). Add butter and stir until melted. Drizzle in cream and stir until fully blended. To serve, divide cake into 6 portions, place in shallow serving bowls and top with generous portions of warm toffee sauce and vanilla custard, ice cream or frozen yogurt.

6 servings

CHILEAN CARICA AND CARDAMOM FROZEN YOGURT

Chilean Carica is a vibrant, golden yellow, exotic fruit that hails from Chili. It resembles papaya in flavor and texture. Combine this with cardamom (related to ginger), with its aromatic, slightly lemony scent and flavor, and blend both with vanilla frozen yogurt and you've got a scrumptious dessert. The first time I prepared this recipe, Nick and I devoured it in one sitting.

This is a great make-ahead, elegant dessert; it's also quite simple to assemble. The yogurt should be soft enough so that you can easily fold in the carica and cardamom; if you let the yogurt get too soft, the fruit will sink to the bottom. Chilean Carica fruit can be found online and in specialty grocery stores. If you can't find carica, replace it with 1 cup of finely chopped ripe mango or papaya.

> *1 quart vanilla frozen yogurt, semi-soft*
> *2 teaspoons ground cardamom*
> *1 cup carica fruit, finely chopped*

In a large bowl, combine semi-soft yogurt with cardamom and carica. Place in a container to accommodate and freeze until serving time.

8 servings

Parsnip Baby Cakes with Ginger Icing

I'm often asked how I come up with my food combinations. I design them in the same way as an architect designs a building: building block by building block, ingredient by ingredient, with a craftsman's sense of the finished product. Food designing, for me, usually occurs after I've awakened in the middle of the night and can't get back to sleep. It's predictably the time when the creative side of my brain gets nudged and when unusual combinations spring to mind: the kind of food combining that might not seem plausible during daylight hours. Here is an unlikely combination where parsnips are added to cake batter. Think about moist carrot cake, and then think about the fact that carrots are cousins to parsnips. No one will ever guess that parsnips are the predominant ingredient in these delicious, moist baby cakes.

1 cup unbleached all-purpose flour
⅔ cup sugar
1 teaspoon baking powder
⅛ teaspoon salt
¼ cup plain yogurt
3 tablespoons canola oil
2 teaspoons grated orange rind
½ teaspoon vanilla
1 egg
1 cup raw parsnips, peeled and shredded

Preheat oven to 350°F. In a large bowl, combine flour, sugar, baking powder and salt. In a medium bowl, whisk together yogurt, oil, orange rind, vanilla and egg. Make a well in the center of dry ingredients, add liquid ingredients and combine until moistened; the batter will be dense. Fold in parsnips, distributing evenly.

Lightly oil 8 muffin cups, distribute batter evenly into cups and bake for 20 minutes or until baby cakes are light brown and toothpick inserted in the center comes out clean. Allow baby cakes to cool for 10 minutes in muffin tin before removing to a wire rack.

Ginger Icing
4 ounces light cream cheese, softened
½ cup confectioners' sugar
1 tablespoon candied ginger
¼ teaspoon vanilla

In a small bowl, combine cream cheese, confectioners' sugar, ginger and vanilla. Beat until mixture is smooth and creamy. When baby cakes have cooled, spread the top of each with icing.

8 baby cakes

CRISPY CREAMY APPLE TURNOVERS

Instead of traditional turnover pastry, wonton wrappers surround these tasty morsels, making them crispy on the outside and creamy on the inside. The cinnamon-sugar topping perfectly complements the apple filling. Just about any variety of apples works in this recipe.

25 wonton wrappers (about half a package)
canola oil for frying
4 ounces light cream cheese, softened
1 medium apple, shredded (peeling is a matter of preference)
a few dashes of salt
½ cup sugar
½ teaspoon cinnamon

In a medium bowl, combine cream cheese, shredded apple and salt. Working with one wonton at a time, place about one teaspoon of the apple/cream cheese filling in the center of a wrapper and fold into a triangular shape. Dampen fingers with water and pinch seams together. As they're assembled, place wontons on a plate, layering wax paper or parchment paper between each layer to prevent wontons from sticking together. Continue filling each wonton wrapper until you have finished using all of the apple/cream cheese mixture. In a large skillet, heat oil over medium-high heat and cook wontons in batches of 5–7 for about 1–2 minutes on each side or until golden brown. In a small bowl, combine sugar and cinnamon. Sprinkle wontons with cinnamon-sugar topping. Serve immediately.

About 25 miniature turnovers

WHIRLED PEACHES WITH AMARETTO

This ridiculously simple-to-prepare dessert soup is perfect to serve when peaches are at the height of their season and plentiful locally. I don't recommend preparing it at any other time of the year. Fresh, juicy, ripe peaches make this soup sing. Light and refreshing, it's a memorable end to any summer meal. For a lovely presentation, serve in chilled martini glasses.

> *6–8 ripe peaches, skins removed, pitted*
> *8 ounces sour cream*
> *¼ cup amaretto almond liqueur*
> *garden-fresh mint leaves (garnish)*

In a blender or food processor, combine peaches, sour cream and amaretto; purée until silky smooth. Chill until ready to serve. Ladle into chilled soup bowls or chilled martini glasses and float a pair of fresh mint leaves on top of each serving.

About eight ½-cup servings

CREAMY CHOCOLATE PUDDING

This is the chocolate lover's version of Very Fruity Pudding (see page 249). It's very satisfying if you're craving chocolate but don't want a high-calorie dessert. If you don't reveal that it's made using tofu as the base, no one will ever know.

>*2 packages (12.3 ounces each) silken extra firm tofu, drained*
>*¼ cup maple syrup*
>*¼ cup agave nectar*
>*2 teaspoons vanilla*
>*½ cup unsweetened cocoa powder*
>*1 teaspoon ground cinnamon*

In a food processor or blender, combine tofu, maple syrup, agave nectar, vanilla, cocoa powder and cinnamon. Purée mixture until smooth and creamy. Refrigerate for several hours before serving.

Eight ½-cup servings

VERY FRUITY PUDDING

A fruity alternative to Creamy Chocolate Pudding (see page 248), this recipe features cherries, but any kind of fruit, fresh or frozen, can be used with great success. The results are delicious, and no one will ever know it's made with tofu.

> *2 packages (12.3 ounces each) Silken Extra Firm Tofu, drained*
> *2 cups fresh or frozen and thawed pitted cherries*
> *¼ cup maple syrup*
> *¼ cup agave nectar*
> *2 teaspoons vanilla*

In a food processor or blender, combine tofu, cherries, maple syrup, agave nectar and vanilla. Purée mixture until smooth and creamy. Refrigerate for several hours before serving.

Ten ½-cup servings

RHUBARB CAKE

When the Eat In-Season Challenge program I founded was launched, I presented this rhubarb cake at a press breakfast that our committee hosted. Rob Kasper, the food editor for Baltimore's primary newspaper, *The Sun*, enthusiastically agreed with Eat In-Season Challenge committee member Martha Lucius' description of this cake as luscious. He loved the cake so much that he ran a story, not only about the challenge, but about rhubarb as well, and he printed this recipe, along with my recipe for Gingered Rhubarb Sauce (see page 41). It is extraordinarily moist, and if I hadn't been the person assembling the ingredients, I would have never guessed that tart-tasting rhubarb was one of the primary ingredients. For optimum results, only make this cake when rhubarb is in season.

2 cups unbleached all-purpose flour
1 teaspoon baking powder
½ teaspoon baking soda
¼ teaspoon cinnamon
⅛ teaspoon salt
½ cup (1 stick) butter, softened
½ cup sugar
½ cup packed brown sugar
1 egg
1 teaspoon vanilla
1 cup buttermilk
2 cups finely diced rhubarb (about ½ pound)
½ cup chopped walnuts
¼ cup packed brown sugar
1½ teaspoons cinnamon

Preheat oven to 350°F. Lightly oil a 13 x 9-inch baking pan. In a medium bowl, combine flour, baking powder, baking soda, cinnamon and salt. In a large bowl, beat butter with white and brown sugar. Add the egg and vanilla and beat until slightly fluffy. Alternately add flour mixture and buttermilk and beat until well combined. Fold in rhubarb. Transfer cake batter to baking pan, spreading evenly. In a small bowl, toss walnuts, brown sugar and cinnamon. Distribute mixture evenly over cake and bake for 35 minutes or until toothpick inserted in center of cake comes out clean.

15 servings

SUMMER'S BERRY BREAD PUDDING

This is a colorful and tasty dish that showcases summer's sweet, nutrient-rich berries. If you're not inclined to prepare homemade whipped cream, crème fraîche, vanilla yogurt, ice cream or custard are also delicious accompaniments. Our favorite is whipped cream, which only takes a few minutes to prepare. Chill the bowl and beaters in the refrigerator for at least 2 hours before whipping the cream.

> 1½ cups coarsely chopped strawberries
> 3½ cups raspberries or blackberries
> 2 cups blueberries
> 1 cup sugar
> ½ cup light Karo corn syrup
> 10–15 slices dense white bread, crusts removed, cubed

In a large saucepan, combine strawberries, 1½ cups raspberries or blackberries, blueberries and sugar. Cook over medium heat until the berries are heated through, about 5 minutes. Remove from heat and cool. In a food processor or blender, combine remaining 2 cups raspberries with syrup and purée until smooth. Place bread cubes in a large bowl and toss with raspberry purée mixture until well distributed. Transfer bread/purée mixture to a lightly oiled 2-quart baking dish. Pour mixed berries evenly over bread, cover and refrigerate overnight.

Allow bread pudding to come to room temperature before baking. Preheat oven to 350°F. Bake for 20–30 minutes or until bubbly. Serve with dollops of whipped cream.

WHIPPED CREAM
> 1 cup heavy whipping cream
> 1 teaspoon vanilla
> 2 tablespoons confectioners' sugar

Beat whipping cream on medium-high speed. When the cream begins to thicken, increase speed slightly and beat until soft peaks form. (Be careful not to over-whip the cream or it will turn to butter.) Fold in vanilla and confectioners' sugar.

6 to 8 servings

STRAWBERRY COBBLER CAKE

When these fire-engine-red gems are in season, I love making this dessert, which is as much a cobbler as it is a cake, hence its name. Serve with Whipped Cream (see page 251), vanilla ice cream or vanilla yogurt.

> *4 cups fresh strawberries, tops removed, washed and quartered*
> *1 cup unbleached all-purpose flour*
> *1 cup sugar*
> *1 teaspoon baking powder*
> *¼ teaspoon salt*
> *4 tablespoons butter, cut into chunks*
> *½ cup milk*
> *1 cup cold water*
> *1 tablespoon cornstarch*

Preheat oven to 350°F. Place berries in a 9-inch round baking dish. In a medium bowl, combine flour, sugar, baking powder and salt. Drop butter chunks into flour mixture. Cut in butter with two knives (making slicing motions) or use your fingertips to incorporate until mixture is somewhat crumbly. Add milk and stir until fully combined. Dollop batter over strawberries (the batter is thick and more like a dough than batter); the final topping and the baking process will evenly distribute the batter. In a medium bowl, combine water and cornstarch. Stir until cornstarch has dissolved and pour over batter. Place baking dish on a rimmed baking sheet and bake cobbler/cake for 45–50 minutes or until lightly browned. Serve warm just as it is or with desired topping.

8 servings

COCONUT LIME CAKE

A bag of limes intended for something else prompted this recipe for a delicious and incredibly moist cake that tastes like it was made with butter and not the canola oil that's used. The consistency of this cake is actually pudding-like: dense and moist beyond belief.

Thai Kitchen produces a great organic coconut milk. To get the most juice from a lime (this applies to all citrus fruits), place it on the counter and roll it back and forth with the palm of your hand.

> *1 can (14 ounces) coconut milk*
> *¾ cup canola oil*
> *½ cup fresh lime juice*
> *2 cups sugar*
> *2½ cups unbleached all-purpose flour*
> *2 eggs*
> *1 teaspoon baking soda*
> *1 cup confectioners' sugar*
> *¼ cup fresh lime juice*
> *7 ounces sweetened coconut*

Preheat oven to 350°F. In a large pot over moderately high heat, whisk together coconut milk, ¾ cup canola oil and lime juice. Heat until mixture is hot to the touch, remove from heat, then stir in sugar. Whisk in flour ½ cup at a time. Add eggs one at a time, whisk until fully blended, then add baking soda. Pour cake batter into a greased 13 x 9-inch baking pan and bake for 30 minutes or until toothpick inserted in center comes out clean. Let cake cool for about 20 minutes before icing.

In a small bowl, combine confectioners' sugar with lime juice and whisk until smooth. Whisk in 1 cup of coconut. Spread icing evenly over top of cake and top icing with remaining coconut.

12 servings

ALMOND SHORTBREAD

This shortbread will melt in your mouth!

> *2 eggs*
> *1 cup sugar*
> *1 cup unbleached all-purpose flour*
> *1 cup (2 sticks) butter, melted*
> *½ cup (1 stick) butter*
> *½ cup sugar*
> *½ cup slivered almonds*
> *1 tablespoon unbleached all-purpose flour*
> *1 tablespoon milk*

Preheat oven to 350°F. Lightly coat a 13 x 9-inch pan with oil. In a medium bowl, whisk eggs, then gradually add sugar, whisking until well blended. Add flour and stir to combine. Stir in melted butter. Spread mixture into prepared pan and bake shortbread for 30 minutes.

In a medium saucepan over moderately low heat, melt butter, then stir in sugar, almonds, flour and milk. Cook until mixture thickens, about 8–15 minutes. Set oven temperature to broil. Pour topping over shortbread and place under broiler for about 1–2 minutes. Watch closely so as not to burn. Allow the shortbread to cool before cutting.

Twenty-four 2-inch squares

PEACH CAKE

The editor of *Urbanite* magazine asked me to develop a recipe for Hoehn's Peach Cake for a feature they were doing on the local bakery and its wildly famous cake. Hoehn's is a Baltimore bakery that has been preparing peach cake from scratch since 1927. Needless to say, I eagerly accepted this challenge and was pleased with the outcome. Prepare this cake when peaches are at the height of their growing season.

> 1¾ cups unbleached all-purpose flour
> ¼ cup sugar
> ½ teaspoon salt
> 1 package active dry yeast
> 2 tablespoons butter, softened
> ½ cup hot water
> 1 egg
> 1½–2 cups peeled and chopped fresh, ripe peaches
> 3 tablespoons sugar
> ¼ teaspoon ground cinnamon
> ½ cup apricot preserves

In a large bowl, combine ½ cup flour, sugar, salt and yeast. Add butter and beat with an electric mixer for a few seconds on medium speed. Gradually add hot water, continuing to beat for 2 minutes on medium speed while scraping the sides of the bowl. Add egg and ½ cup flour, switch to high speed and beat for 2 minutes, scraping the sides of the bowl. Stir in remaining ¾ cup flour and mix until well blended. Lightly coat a 9-inch round pan with oil and spread batter into pan. (Batter will be thick and sticky, so don't be concerned if you can't spread it evenly. The rising process will evenly distribute the mixture.) Top the batter with chopped peaches. In a small bowl combine sugar and cinnamon. Sprinkle over peaches. Cover with plastic wrap and allow to rise in a warm, draft-free place until double in bulk, about 1 hour.

Preheat oven to 400°F. Bake cake for 25 minutes. Allow the cake to cool for 10 minutes before carefully transferring to a rimmed serving platter. Heat apricot preserves in a small saucepan over low heat. Spoon warm preserves evenly over cake.

8 servings

OH, MY! SHORTBREAD

"Decadent," is what taste-testers said after sampling these buttery morsels; they're guaranteed to disappear within minutes. A box grater or food processor with a shredder attachment can be used to grate the dough. If you are using a food processor, form the dough into logs that are the circumference of the feed tube.

> *2 cups unbleached all-purpose flour*
> *1 teaspoon baking powder*
> *½ teaspoon salt*
> *1 cup (2 sticks) butter, softened*
> *1 cup sugar*
> *2 egg yolks*
> *1 teaspoon vanilla*
> *¾ cup preserves (apricot, raspberry, strawberry or your preference)*

In a medium bowl, combine flour, baking powder and salt. In a large bowl, using an electric mixer, beat the butter and sugar until well combined. Add egg yolks and vanilla and beat until incorporated. Add the flour mixture and beat until a dough forms. Shape the dough into logs, wrap in plastic wrap and refrigerate for several hours or overnight.

Preheat oven to 350°F. Grate half of the dough and place into a generously oiled 11 x 7-inch or 2-liter glass baking dish. Do not pat or press the dough into the pan. Drop spoonfuls of the preserves over the surface of the dough (do not spread; the preserves will evenly distribute during baking). Grate remaining dough and top preserves with grated dough; do not press down. Bake for about 30 minutes. Switch oven temperature to broil and lightly brown the top of the shortbread. Watch carefully; it will brown very quickly. Allow the shortbread to cool completely before cutting into squares.

About 20 squares

What to buy • *Where to buy* • *Why to buy*

PRODUCT RESOURCE LIST

Agave nectar

While agave has been used for thousands of years as an ingredient in food, it is only now becoming the preferred sweetener used by doctors, natural food enthusiasts, and health-conscious consumers (due to increasing awareness of agave nectar's many beneficial properties). Agave nectar can be found at health-oriented grocery stores or you can purchase it online. For more information, log on to www.allaboutagave.com.

Artichokes

Artichokes are only picked when ripe, so they're ready to cook when you see them in the supermarket. Look for firm, compact, round artichokes that are heavy for their size. Avoid the ones with leaves that are dry, yellowish or spreading apart. You can tell if an artichoke is fresh and moist if it squeaks when you squeeze it.

Avocado, ripening

A ripe avocado should be dark green to black and will yield to gentle pressure. If an avocado isn't ripe, it may take 1–5 days to ripen. To hasten the ripening process, place avocados in a brown paper bag. Do not refrigerate.

Baking powder

There are some baking powders on the market that contain aluminum. Look for aluminum-free baking powder, which can be found in most major supermarkets.

Beef flavored broth, organic

Imagine brand Organic Beef Flavored Broth is made from real beef and the finest ingredients: a zesty combination of fresh, organic herbs and savory spices. Imagine Foods can be found in most health-oriented grocery stores. For more information on Imagine Foods, visit their website www.imaginefoods.com.

Butcher's twine/kitchen string

Butcher's twine can be used to tie roasts so that they keep their shape, to secure the legs of poultry for roasting or, as I've used it, to tie the butterflied pork loin in my recipe for Bourbon Pork with Creamy Mustard Sauce (see page 161). I recommend using only 100% biodegradable cotton twine/string. Kitchen twine or string can be found in most kitchen-oriented stores, in independent hardware stores or in the hardware department of retail stores.

Cast-iron cookware

Many of the recipes in *Tasting the Seasons* were prepared using cast-iron cookware. Non-stick coatings on pots and pans can release toxic fumes; well-seasoned cast-iron cookware cooks food beautifully, without the worry of toxicity. Cooks have relied on this versatile and affordable cookware for hundreds of years. If you care for it properly it will last for decades. Cast-iron pots and pans can often be found at yard sales, antique stores, flea-markets and Whole Foods Market. Sometimes cast-iron has been neglected (look for rust spots) and will need to be revived. Remove rust spots with steel wool. Preheat oven to 350°F, generously coat the cookware with canola oil and bake for 20 minutes. Continue this oiling/baking process until the cookware becomes well seasoned. The test to determine if your cookware is well seasoned is that after cooking something on the sticky side (eggs, stir-fry, etc.) the cookware behaves as if it's nonstick. To care for cast-iron, wash with water and use dish detergent or soap sparingly. Dry and coat with a thin coating of oil.

Ceramic cookware

Our teapot is made by Ceramcor, the makers of Xtrema Ceramic Cookware, a patented ceramic product that's 100% green, environmentally safe and non-toxic. It's made of natural minerals and water and handcrafted by skilled artisans. To find out more, visit Ceramcor online at www. ceramcor.com.

Cheeses

Asadero: (pronounced ah-sah-DARE-oh) An off-white, semi-firm Mexican cheese with a mildly tangy taste and a creamy texture. Asadero means "roasting" or "roaster" in Spanish. It's great for melting and a favorite when making quesadillas. Also known as Oaxaca and Chihuahua cheese, Asadero can be found in most gourmet cheese departments.

Feta: Probably the best known Greek cheese and, some say, the national cheese of Greece. Traditional Greek feta is soft in texture, rich in aroma and tangy in flavor, while French feta cheese tends to be milder, creamier and less salty. My favorite feta is Valbreso French Feta Cheese, which can be found in most grocery stores.

Halloumi: (pronounced hah-LOO-me) One of my all-time favorite food discoveries. Halloumi is a semi-soft cheese that is closely associated with Cyprus and the Middle East. This cheese is incredibly versatile; it can be grilled, roasted, fried or eaten fresh. And it has a mild, creamy, slightly salty taste that pairs well with a wide range of foods. When halloumi is grilled, it develops a rich, golden crust, and while it softens, it does not melt. It also holds its shape when fried.

Pecorino Romano: From the word *pecora* which means "ewe" in Italian, cheeses made from sheep's milk in Italy are called pecorino. The best-known pecorino is Pecorino Romano. Genuine Romano is only produced in the province of Rome from November to June. Look for the sheep's head logo with Pecorino Romano embossed on the rind.

Robiola: (pronounced roh-bee-OH-lah) This creamy fresh cheese from Italy is often used for cooking, and it's great on pizza. It's also served as an antipasto along with olive oil and/or fresh herbs. There are many robiolas that can be found in specialty cheese shops or Whole Foods Market. I particularly like the flavor and extraordinarily creamy texture in robiola due latti, made using part cow's milk and part sheep's milk.

Chicken broth

When I was growing up, I remember my mother making the most memorable soups and stews using her homemade chicken broth. I fully endorse homemade broth, but if time is of essence, Imagine Organic Free Range Chicken Broth is a full-bodied chicken broth that comes closest to the flavor of the broth my mother prepared. Imagine Organic Free Range Chicken Broth can be found at most grocery stores, or you can find a store near you by logging on to their website www.imaginefoods.com.

Chilean Carica

Also known as Chilean Papaya, Golden Papaya and Chilean Mountain Papaya, this boutique fruit is an extremely versatile gourmet product. Chilean Carica from Tamaya Gourmet enhances any dish, from a simple appetizer to a green salad, a cold or hot dish, a special dessert or even an exotic drink or juice. Beautifully packed in a glass jar, it makes a great hostess gift. Visit www.tamayagourmet.com.

Christmas lima beans

A true lima bean, (originally from Peru, hence "Lima") this gorgeous bean has all the "meat" of limas but with a chestnut flavor. Heirloom Beans Christmas lima beans are available at Whole Foods Market, or you can buy them online from Rancho Gordo New World Specialty Food. Log on to their website at www.ranchogordo.com to find a variety of Heirloom Beans.

Corn, de-cobbing

Buy corn at the height of its growing season when it's most plentiful and delicious. Cook large quantities, de-cob and then freeze for year-round use. After you've cooked the corn and allowed it to cool, place a rimmed baking sheet in the sink. Cut the tip of the cob to create a flat end. With a sharp paring knife (starting from the top) slice the corn as close to the cob as possible (you can usually cut about 4 rows at a time), removing corn until you've reached the bottom of the cob. Do this until you've finished removing all the kernels from the cob. With the dull side of the paring knife, use the same technique to extract the heart of the kernel from the cob. I freeze corn in one- and two-cup portions (it can be a bit difficult to separate fresh corn once frozen into portions). This helps when you need a certain measurement in recipes.

Couscous

Cooked and served like rice, couscous is actually small granules of pasta. I recommend Near East Couscous Mix, especially my favorite variety, Toasted Pine Nut. Near East products are found nationwide in supermarkets. For more information, visit them online at www.neareast.com.

Cream of mushroom soup

Amy's Organic Soups Semi-Condensed Cream of Mushroom is available from Whole Foods Market and most health-oriented grocery stores. For more information on products from Amy's Kitchen, visit them online at www.amyskitchen.com.

Flax seeds

Flax seeds come whole or ground; my preference is to grind my own whole seeds for optimum flavor and nutritional value. I've tested many brands and found that I prefer Premium Gold Whole Flax Seed for its freshness. I also endorse this North Dakota-based, independently owned company's philosophy about farming and food. Flax seeds can be found in most health-oriented grocery stores. For more information, log on to www.flaxpremiumgold.com.

Flour, chestnut

Allen Creek Farm (located in Washington state) generally has this flour in stock year-round. Go to www.chestnutsonline.com.

French onion dip mix

Simply Organic makes a wonderful French onion dip mix. The Simply Organic brand is available at Whole Foods Market and other natural foods stores, as well as mainstream supermarkets. For your nearest retailer, go to www.simplyorganicfoods.com.

French press

Every time you brew a pot of coffee in a plastic coffee maker, dioxins are released into the air—carcinogens highly toxic to cells in our bodies. We switched to using a French press (Bodum) to prepare our coffee. For more information about this eco-coffee essential, visit www.bodum.com.

Fruit, canned

When a recipe calls for canned fruit, I recommend using Oregon Fruit Products, www.oregonfruit.com. I love the quality and the philosophy behind this family-owned company. The product tastes so pure and fresh. To find a store in your area, go to their website.

Ginger, fresh

Fresh ginger should have smooth skin and be a uniformly buff color. Ginger is a root and typically has lots of knobs: the fewer knobs, the easier to remove the peel.

Hibiscus tea
Nile Valley Herbs makes a delicious organic hibiscus mint tea. To find out more about Nile Valley Teas and to order online, visit their website www.nilevalleyherbs.com.

Hot buttered rum mix
The Spice Hunter Winter Sippers Hot Buttered Rum Mix is a complementary blend of brown sugar, cinnamon, nutmeg, cardamom, allspice, cloves and lemon oil. It is available from Whole Foods Market and most specialty grocery stores during the Thanksgiving and Christmas holiday season, or visit their website where you can order their products online www.spicehunter.com.

Mango, ripening
A ripe mango will yield to slight pressure. If you can't find a ripe one, place the mango in a paper bag. Keep at room temperature until the flesh yields, which can take several days. To get the flesh of the mango, slice the mango lengthwise on both sides as close to the pit as possible. Crisscross-cut the pulpy side of each piece and then turn inside out by holding each half with both hands and pushing in on the skin side. (Think about turning an orange or lemon wedge inside out.) Once you've got the fruit exposed, cut the mango from the skin. You can get some additional fruit from the top and bottom of the remaining section of mango, the section containing the pit.

Mayonnaise
The expeller-pressed canola oil mayonnaise distributed by Whole Foods Market is the mayonnaise used for the recipes in this cookbook. I really like its close-to-homemade flavor.

Molasses
I tested several brands and found that molasses is one of the most variable products. My favorite, and the one that is used in *Tasting the Seasons*, is a special blend (from a special family recipe) that comes from a small market on the eastern shore of Maryland. Old Time Barrel Molasses is a true artisanal company. They have no website, just an excellent product with a handwritten label Scotch-taped to the Mason jar it comes in.

Old Time Barrel Molasses can be ordered by contacting:
Simmons Center Market
600 Race Street
Cambridge, MD 21613
410-228-4313

Mushrooms, storage and preparation

Mushrooms are best kept in the refrigerator in a loosely closed paper bag; plastic suffocates and bruises mushrooms. Despite other opinions, I recommend washing mushrooms. Just prior to preparing, gently wash mushrooms and place on an absorbent kitchen towel and pat dry.

Pasta

I appreciate the efforts of Bionaturae, an organic pasta producer, to produce a delicious noodle. They mix the semolina with spring water; it is then pressed with antique bronze dye, a technique that gives it a coarse surface that better absorbs sauce. The pasta is dried slowly and naturally, and this process preserves the original nutrients (www.bionaturae.com).

Preserves

Cherry, Raspberry, Strawberry: Bonne Maman produces wonderful preserves in a variety of flavors. You can find Bonne Maman products at most major grocery stores.

Plum: McCutcheon's Damson Plum Preserves is my plum preserve of preference. These preserves can often be found at farmers markets or online at www.mccutcheons.com.

Pudding

Kozy Shack brand makes a delicious, homemade Chocolate All Natural Pudding. It can be found in the refrigerated section (near dairy) at most grocery stores.

Pumpkin Pie in a Jar

Pumpkin Pie in a Jar is a combination of the flavors you adore in a flavorful pumpkin pie, with familiar spices like cinnamon, nutmeg and allspice that traditionally enhance pumpkin. Look for it at your local specialty foods store during the autumn and winter months.

Salba

Salba is a nutritional grain that is naturally rich in omega-3, fiber, antioxidants, vitamins and minerals. It comes whole or ground, and either one produces a welcome crunch when added to recipes. Salba can be found in health-oriented grocery stores.

Salt

My favorite multi-purpose salt is Redmond Real Salt. It is available in powder, granular, kosher, and coarse grinds. Salt that is white has been bleached: salt in its natural form should have a grayish color with some specks of red. Redmond Real Salt can be found in most health-oriented grocery stores or go to their website www.realsalt.com.

Sauerkraut

I recommend Great Lakes Kraut Company's Silver Floss Traditional Shredded Sauerkraut, and for good reason: it won the American Culinary ChefsBest award. Silver Floss Sauerkraut can be found in most grocery stores.

Shortening

Spectrum Organic All Vegetable Shortening can be found in most health-oriented grocery stores or go to www.spectrumorganics.com.

Shrimp, steamed

I think the most flavorful shrimp comes from shrimp you steam, peel and devein. The true shrimp flavor that comes from the shell is extracted during the cooking process. If this method seems too time consuming, the next best choice is shrimp marked "easy peel." It comes raw with shell and tail on, but it's been deveined.

Simply Organic

Simply Organic makes a wonderful French onion dip mix, taco seasoning and Southwest taco seasoning. The Simply Organic brand is currently available at Whole Foods Market and other natural foods stores, as well as mainstream supermarkets. For more about Simply Organic products go to www.simplyorganicfoods.com.

Soba noodles

Soba noodles are native Japanese pasta made of buckwheat flour (*soba-ko*) and wheat flour (*komugi-ko*). Soba are thin, spaghetti-like noodles made of buckwheat flour that, because it doesn't bind well, is often combined with wheat flour or yam. According to Japanese agricultural regulations, soba must contain at least 30 percent buckwheat; the higher the buckwheat content, the better the noodles, and the nuttier the flavor. There are several variations of these noodles: 100% Whole Buckwheat and Wild Yam (*Jinenjo*). They can be found at Whole Foods Market and in the international section of most health food stores. (Eden Foods soba noodles are found most everywhere.)

Spices

For optimum flavor, spices should be fresh. Any spices you have had more than a year should be discarded. Keep jarred spices closed and away from heat (the worst place—albeit most common— is above the stove), light and moisture. For quick and easy accessibility, alphabetize spices or arrange them based on how frequently you use them. For spices you use infrequently, it's best to purchase the smallest quantity available. Buy spices packaged in glass jars. Avoid spices that have been irradiated or carry the Radura symbol (Eco-Tips-Eco-Terms-Eco-Techniques, see page 269). Food labels are required by law to say whether the spice has been irradiated. To learn more about irradiation and become familiar with the Radura symbol, visit www.sustainabletable.org.

Tamari soy sauce
Similar to, but slightly thicker than soy sauce, tamari soy sauce is made from soybeans and a small amount of wheat. It has a mellower flavor than soy sauce. I often use it instead of soy sauce (made using larger amounts of wheat), but it can also be used as a dipping sauce or for basting. Because it is nearly wheat free (wheat-free tamari is available as well), it's a good choice for those with wheat allergies.

Teff
Teff is not only the smallest grain in the world, it is also one of the most nutritious. Teff flour is a very good source of dietary fiber, protein and iron. It is also gluten-free. It can be found in health-oriented grocery stores.

This Book Cooks
Tasting the Seasons references several recipes found in my first cookbook, *This Book Cooks*. The references are merely suggesting complementing dishes. If you don't have a copy of *This Book Cooks* and would like to purchase it, you can order it online or from your local book store or directly from me. The book has nearly 200 user-friendly recipes from appetizers to desserts.

Tofu, Mori-Nu Silken Extra Firm Tofu
As opposed to the tofu found in the refrigerated section, this can be found in the non-refrigerated section of most health-oriented grocery stores.

Tomato Cinnamon Clove Preserves
Tomato Cinnamon Clove Preserves is one of many food products created by A Perfect Pear from Napa Valley, the only pear-focused gourmet condiment company in the country. You can buy directly from A Perfect Pear or find a store in your area by logging on to their website at www. aperfectpear.com.

Tomatoes, canned
I recommend using Muir Glen Organic Tomatoes. Since their founding in 1991, they've been committed to helping farmers choose to grow tomatoes organically. All of Muir Glen's tomatoes are field grown and vine ripened under certified organic practices—no synthetic pesticides, no chemical fertilizers, just gorgeous tomato taste, true to nature.

Tomatoes, fresh
For optimum flavor, it's best to keep tomatoes out of the refrigerator (this applies to cherry tomatoes as well). When slicing, chopping or dicing tomatoes (or any messy fruit or vegetable), place a rimmed baking sheet under the cutting board to keep juices from running over the counter. To blanch and remove skin from tomatoes, cut an X on the bottom of the tomato, plunge into boiling water for 30 seconds, and remove using a slotted spoon. Allow tomatoes to cool before coring and removing skin.

Vegetable bouillon cubes
If you're a vegan, a vegetarian or just someone who loves vegetable bouillon straight or as a base for soups, sauces, etc., I recommend Rapunzel Vegan Vegetable Bouillon with Sea Salt. Rapunzel offers a line of full-bodied vegan vegetable bouillon cubes, and while I prefer the regular with sea salt, they also make one with herbs and another with no salt added. Rapunzel products (www. rapunzel.com) are available at most health-oriented grocery stores and Whole Foods Market.

Vegetable juice
R.W. Knudsen Family, Very Veggie Organic Vegetable Juice is the authentic-tasting, tomato-based vegetable juice I prefer to use. Knudsen can be found in most health-oriented grocery stores.

Vinegars
Apple cider vinegar is a kitchen staple and has a myriad of culinary uses. The organic, unfiltered brands (used in this cookbook) have a more robust, authentic apple cider vinegar flavor. Seasoned rice vinegar has a light, tangy, slightly sweet flavor.

Zester/grater
The Microplane Zester/Grater shaves the zest from citrus fruits (as well as chocolate and hard cheeses) in a way that's impossible to duplicate with a knife. This handy culinary tool is available from most kitchen-oriented stores.

ECO-TERMS-ECO-TIPS-ECO-TECHNIQUES

Artisanal movement
This movement supports products (foods and drinks) that are produced, for lack of a better term, the old-fashioned way: using traditional methods, often hand-crafted by artisans/artists from family-owned farms or stores.

Carbon footprint
A carbon footprint is the total amount of greenhouse gas emissions (measured in units of carbon dioxide) that is released into the environment over a given period of time.

Community Supported Agriculture, CSA
Over the last 20 years, Community Supported Agriculture (CSA) has become a popular way for consumers to buy local, seasonal food directly from a farmer. Here are the basics: a farmer offers a certain number of shares to the public. Typically, a share entitles you to vegetables, but other farm products may be included. Interested consumers purchase a share (a membership or a subscription) and in return, receive a container of seasonal produce each week throughout the farming season.

Composting
Composting is the process of combining unwanted yard waste, clean food waste and other organic materials (under controlled conditions) so that the original raw ingredients are transformed into rich compost (completely decayed organic matter that is rich in nutrients and used for conditioning soil). If you haven't set in motion this wonderful giving-back-to-the-earth function, you may want to look into the possibilities of composting in your yard or neighborhood. There are all sorts of wonderful sites to refer to but I especially like *Composting 101: A Composting Guide for the Home Gardener*. It's a friendly site, complete and concise. For more information, visit www.composting101.com.

Food seasons
As a frequent food shopper, I watch in frustration as consumers load grocery carts with foods that are clearly out of season. I've watched many shoppers stocking their carts with asparagus, zucchini, honeydew melon, strawberries, blueberries and blackberries in January. Everything was months (at the very least) from being in season. You've probably never heard of a corn eating contest in January, or a strawberry festival in October and it would be hard to envision ruby red tomatoes ripening on the vine in your garden the morning after a winter snowstorm has blown in. That's because these concepts go against nature. Growing, harvesting and buying foods out of their season does more than tax the environment; it also throws our bodies out of synch with nature.

On average, the food we eat travels 2,000 miles. With each passing mile, the quality, freshness and nutritional value found in just-harvested fruits and vegetables diminish. However, if we buy only locally grown food (or food produced within a 150-mile radius of our home) we're working with nature, helping the environment and supporting local farmers. Just-harvested food is at its peak of flavor and provides optimum nutrition. To find out what's in season in your area, visit the Natural Resources Defense Council's website at www.nrdc.org. Once there, click on Green Living > Green Living Guides > Eat Local.

Food wraps

I can remember my grandmother using wax paper to wrap cheeses and sandwiches and to cover freshly prepared dishes. Today there are more types of food wrappings on the market than she could ever have imagined. In order to help our planet, look for eco-friendly unbleached wax paper and unbleached parchment paper. When you need to use foil, use 100% recycled. Try to wean yourself off of potentially harmful food coverings. If you use plastic wrap, use it sparingly.

Fresh fruits and vegetables

The Dirty Dozen and The Clean Fifteen
The Environmental Working Group (EWG) is a non-profit organization that advocates health and environmental protection. After studying data from the U.S. Department of Agriculture and the U.S. Food and Drug Administration, the group came up with two lists: The Dirty Dozen and The Clean Fifteen, noting the highest and lowest concentrations of pesticide residues in certain produce.

The Dirty Dozen
This list contains the fruits and vegetables most contaminated by exposure to pesticides. It is recommended that consumers only buy this produce when it has been grown organically. Listed in order of contamination—highest to lowest.

Peaches, Apples, Bell Peppers, Celery, Nectarines, Strawberries, Cherries, Kale, Lettuce, Grapes (Imported), Carrots, Pears

If you can't memorize The Dirty Dozen, here's a good rule of thumb to follow: select organic for any fruits and vegetables with thin or fragile skin or surfaces that "grab." Friendlier to eat are The Clean Fifteen. This list contains the fruits and vegetables that register the lowest levels of pesticide contamination.

The Clean Fifteen
Though this produce registers lower on the contamination scale, washing is still recommended. Listed with the cleanest first.

Onions, Avocados, Sweet Corn (Frozen), Pineapple, Mango, Asparagus, Sweet Peas (Frozen), Kiwifruit, Cabbage, Eggplant, Papaya, Watermelon, Broccoli, Tomatoes, Sweet Potatoes

Regardless of which list your favorite produce appears on, I would offer you the same advice. When preparing fruits and vegetables for consumption, buy organic and wash everything. Buy as much locally grown food as possible. Food intended for local markets, as well as food provided directly from a local farmer, have typically been exposed to fewer chemicals because there is less need to artificially control freshness and ripening time.

Freezing Summer's Bounty
It's simple to freeze many of summer's fruits, especially blueberries, raspberries, blackberries and strawberries. (They're great to use in fruit smoothies.) Remember that all food slated for freezing should be frozen when it's very fresh, rather than just before it looks like it's about to go bad. Gently wash the berries and arrange the berries in a single layer on a cookie sheet. Place in the freezer for a few hours. Once they're frozen solid, transfer to an eco-friendly freezer bag. Remember that flash-freezing locks in nutrients, so whether you're doing the freezing yourself or buying fruit that's already been frozen, it's perfectly acceptable.

Household cleaners
You can depend on the Natural Products Association if you question which household cleaners are truly green. Home-care items, including household cleaners and detergents, carry the natural seal (green leaf inside a house) if they don't contain ingredients that harm health or the environment. Manufacturing processes can't include harsh chemicals. Furthermore, products can never be tested on animals, and products that carry the seal use sustainable packaging.

Irradiation
A lot of our food is being irradiated (exposed to high doses of radiation in the form of gamma rays, X-rays or electron beams) in order to extend the food's shelf life. Foods currently approved for irradiation by the U.S. Food and Drug Administration include meat and poultry, eggs, fruits and vegetables, juices, herbs, spices and flour. Since 1986, all irradiated products must carry the international symbol called a *radura*, a green, circular logo that resembles a stylized flower. There is so much to learn about the irradiation of our food and the consequences to our planet: www. sustainabletable.org is an informative website.

Kitchen management
Poor kitchen management is costly, and it taxes the environment. Get to know what you have in your pantry and refrigerator before you go shopping. To prevent waste and over-buying, clean out your refrigerator once a week. Keep a running grocery list. Food is not meant to be wasted; it's meant to be consumed. On average, an American household wastes 14% of its food purchases. And it's not just the food that's being wasted; think of all the water and energy that

went into producing, packaging and transporting all of those wasted items. Purchase only the amount you are able to consume, and compost all clean food waste.

Natural Resources Defense Council, NRDC
The mission of the NRDC is to safeguard the Earth: its people, its plants, animals, and the natural systems on which all life depends. The council aims to do the following: to restore the integrity of the elements that sustain life—air, land, and water—and to defend endangered natural places, to establish sustainability and good stewardship of the Earth as central ethical imperatives of human society, to affirm the integral place of human beings in the environment, to protect nature in ways that will advance the long-term welfare of present and future generations, to foster the fundamental right of all people to have a voice in decisions affecting their environment, and to break down the pattern of disproportionate environmental burdens borne by people of color and others who face social or economic inequities. Ultimately, NRDC strives to help create a new way of life for humankind, one that can be sustained indefinitely without fouling or depleting the resources that support all life on Earth. To learn more, visit www.nrdc.org.

Organic
Organic foods are produced without using fertilizers made with synthetic ingredients, sewage sludge, synthetic pesticides, ionizing radiation or bioengineering. Organic meat, poultry, dairy and eggs come from animals that are raised on organic feed and are free of growth hormones and antibiotics.

In organic farming, the soil is nurtured from the addition of organic matter (combining composted material with soil for optimum balance, water conservation and proper nutrient levels), rotating crops, and planting beneficial cover crops. In conventional farming, soil is replenished with synthetic additives and chemicals.

If you want to reduce your exposure to harmful pesticides and are interested in sustaining the health of our planet, it is best to choose organic.

Pre-packaged, pre-pared food
It seems that more and more food is being sold as pre-something. Cheese is pre-shredded and pre-sliced, fruit and vegetables are pre-washed and pre-cut, and meats are pre-cooked and pre-sliced. It's all intended to be convenient, except pre-shredding, pre-slicing, pre-washing, pre-cutting and pre-cooking sacrifices so much of the flavor naturally found in the food. Once food is taken from its whole being (as in shredded, cut or sliced) it loses many of its beneficial nutrients.

Produce labels and what they reveal
The numbers on the little stickers that you find on almost every piece of grocery store produce reveal more than you might imagine. According to the International Federation for Produce Standards, a four-digit code means the item is conventionally grown, most likely with

pesticides and fertilizers. A five-digit code starting with 8 means the produce is genetically modified. And a five-digit code starting with 9 means the produce was organically grown. For example, if an apple has the code 6584 on the sticker, that apple would have been grown from unaltered seed with the possible use of fertilizers and pesticides. An apple labeled 86584 would be genetically altered. And an apple with a code reading 96584 would have been grown organically.

Recycling

Recycling takes a used product and turns it into something that can be used again. Recycled products are made from fibers and/or materials that we once considered waste. Although most products have the potential to be recycled, not all do. Most communities have recycling programs that collect specific items.

Bottles, containers and packaging made of plastic are typically stamped or embossed with a symbol, a number (1–7) and/or an acronym or letters. Although the presence of the symbol implies that the plastic item is recyclable, in actuality, the branding is only intended to identify the plastic resin from which the item was made. Below is a brief description of what to look for on plastic items and what the branding means.

#1 PET (or PETE) – Widely recycled; used for beverage containers. **#2 HDPE** – Widely recycled; used for milk containers and grocery bags. **#3 VINYL or PVC** – Cannot be recycled. **#4 LDPE** – Recyclable at drop-off centers; used for plastic film and produce bags. **#5 PP** – Recyclable in some areas; used for yogurt containers. **#6 PS** – Rarely recyclable; used for coffee cups, serving plates and dishes. **#7 Miscellaneous: PLA and PC** – Compostable PLA can be sent to a municipal facility, but PC (polycarbonate) is neither compostable nor recyclable.

Shopping bags, reusable

Most grocery stores sell reusable grocery bags. Store them in a visible place so you don't forget them. I split my bags up; some are in the trunk of the car, others are in the kitchen close to the grocery list. Unbleached cotton net bags with drawstrings that are available at health-oriented grocery stores and Whole Foods Markets are great for toting fruits and vegetables. I recommend periodically washing grocery bags to remove any bacteria. I wash them with my kitchen towels and oven mitts on a gentle cycle.

Slow Food

Slow Food is a non-profit, global grassroots movement that was founded in 1989 to counteract fast food and fast living. By linking the pleasures of food with a commitment to community and the environment, Slow Food addresses people's dwindling interest in the food they eat and how it tastes, knowing where it comes from and understanding that their food choices affect the rest of the world. To find out more about the Slow Food movement, visit their website www. slowfood.com.

Sustainability

Sustainability is the practice of using resources in an efficient and responsible manner to protect the environment and allow continued economic growth and development of social equity. It is a way of giving consideration to future generations.

Sustainable Table

This program was created in 2003 by the non-profit organization GRACE to help consumers understand the problems with our food supply and offer viable solutions and alternatives. Sustainable Table celebrates local sustainable food, educates consumers on food-related issues and works to build community through the joy of food and eating. Visit their website at www. sustainabletable.org.

INDEX

cocoa, *cont.*:
    creamy chocolate pudding, 248
    rolled chocolate pudding cake, 236

coconut:
    coconut lime cake, 253
    coconut peanut wafers, 18
    curried carrot soup with coconut shrimp, 86
    Indian meatball stew with curried cucumber yogurt, 81-82

coconut milk:
    coconut lime cake, 253
    coconut peanut wafers, 18
    curried carrot soup with coconut shrimp, 86
    gingered coconut carrot soup, 106
    gingered parsnip and coconut soup, 88

coffeecake:
    cherry almond coffee cake, 56
    mango and cardamom coffee cake with almond streusel, 73

coleslaw:
    kohlrabi coleslaw, 180

cookies:
    caramel-centered chocolate cookies, 239
    cinnamon ginger cookies, 234

corn, fresh:
    a maize zing corn pudding, 194
    bowl of summer's bounty, 109
    cheese tortellini chowder, 95
    cold crab and corn soup, 104
    corn chowder, 119
    southwest taco beef with cornbread crust, 158
    summer's harvest soup, 110-111
    product resource list, 259

cornmeal:
    cranberry walnut muffins, 61
    dual-seed cornmeal bread, 218
    golden bread, 222

cornmeal, *cont.*:
    hot-buttered-rum pumpkin biscuits, 216
    mushroom and robiola cheese polenta pie, 201
    nutrient-rich breakfast muffins, 68
    peach pancakes, 70
    plum perfect pancakes, 66
    powerhouse blueberry waffles, 57
    southwest taco beef with cornbread crust, 158

couscous:
    berry nutty couscous, 208
    product resource list, 260

crabmeat:
    bowl of summer's bounty, 109
    cold crab and corn soup, 104
    crab cakes, 125
    crab fritters, 12
    creamy crab soup, 117
    imperial crab imperial, 129

cracker crumbs:
    crab cakes, 125
    imperial crab imperial, 129
    see also bread crumbs

cranberries:
    berry nutty couscous, 208
    cranberry apple salad with sunflower seeds, 175
    cranberry walnut muffins, 61
    fruity, nutty, blue-cheesy spinach salad, 179
    honeyed pecan salad with tangerine vinaigrette, 174
    maté chai latte muffins, 65
    nutrient-rich breakfast muffins, 68
    raspberry orange cranberry sauce, 38

cranberry-raspberry juice:
    raspberry orange cranberry sauce, 38

cream, half-and-half, heavy whipping cream:
    bowl of summer's bounty, 109
    carrot and leek gratin, 207

ABOUT THE AUTHOR

Kerry Dunnington's passion for creative preparation of foods in their growing season, ethical food practices and healthy food consumption encompasses all that she's done for three decades as a food columnist, recipe developer, entertainment consultant, culinary judge and award-winning cookbook author.

She maintains a keen focus on supporting local farmers, promoting sustainable and organic growing and harvesting methodologies. In her talks and writings, she shares her passion with her audiences as she encourages them to purchase food and prepare menus that are not only healthful and delicious, but involve reduced transportation miles and a smaller carbon footprint.

Kerry writes for multiple publications, including the *Examiner* newspapers, *Smart Woman*, *baltimore eats*, and the *Urbanite*. A life-long eco-stylist and food enthusiast, she serves on the Chef's Council and the Board of the American Institute of Wine and Food and is founder of Slow Food Baltimore's "Eat in Season Challenge." She frequently serves the Mid-Atlantic region with her food judging, cooking demonstrations, and culinary/cuisine presentations.

Her newest book, *Tasting the Seasons,* includes an impressive variety of fast and fresh, irresistible, user-friendly recipes—family-oriented, one-dish wonders, updated classics, and creative gourmet entrees—all presented with a steady focus on how to identify, select, and prepare foods using ecologically sound principles. Her creative flair in the kitchen and in her writing is seen in her narratives preceding each recipe.

After receiving countless rave reviews for her first cookbook, *This Book Cooks*, now in its second edition, Kerry began compiling the contents of *Tasting the Seasons*. She is now hard at work on her third cookbook.

In addition to writing cookbooks, Kerry has been operating a busy cottage-style catering service for decades from her home in the Tuscany-Canterbury neighborhood of Baltimore, which she shares with her husband (and official taste-tester), Nick Dunnington. When she isn't preparing food for clients, her daily rounds are filled with compiling food combinations that she turns into recipes. Now living the concepts of "local, organic and sustainable," Kerry continues her writing on this subject.

COMING SOON: THE NEW EDITION OF "THIS BOOK COOKS"

In the new edition of *This Book Cooks*, readers will discover lively, useful, new and inspiring introductory material, a comprehensive index, and a stylish, user-friendly format. *This Book Cooks* is completely accessible, easy to navigate, and it's an inspirational cover-to-cover culinary read. This updated version also includes engaging illustrations, revised recipes and most notably, enriched storytelling about Kerry's life growing up around food.

Originally published in 2004, *This Book Cooks* became an instant classic for the home cook. The new edition has a stronger nod toward the farm-fresh approach in an effort to preserve and share the author's childhood memories of food. The book will help to influence future generations about the importance of implementing family food traditions, shopping the harvest, appreciating the bounty, and sharing in the goodness and nourishment that home life and nature offers us. Divided into nine chapters, by course from appetizers to desserts (including a chapter devoted to recipes for dog treats!), *This Book Cooks* offers a rich collection of award-winning recipes.

A must-have volume you can depend upon for all your culinary needs, *This Book Cooks* promises to:

- Inspire you to cook,
- Make your everyday eating and entertaining easier as well as more enjoyable,
- Supply you with a vast choice of simple, crowd-pleasing recipes you will come back to again and again.

NOTES

19.95

11/17/14.